Building Communities of Trust

Drawing upon a combination of ethnographic research and media and communication theory, Building Communities of Trust: *Creative Work for Social Change* offers pathways to building trust in a range of situations and communities.

Ann Feldman presents rich examples from her own life and social-impact journey with nonprofit Artistic Circles, along with supplemental case studies from interviews with 20- to 30-year-olds, to address how to create vibrant, trust-based societies and to determine what works and what doesn't work while creating social impact. These case studies and shared experiences from real-life media projects across 30 years reveal behind-the-scenes stories of challenges, conflicts, and resolutions in global impact efforts ranging from women's empowerment to water access. The book explains how the success—or failure—of social-impact initiatives depends on power struggles, funding, interpersonal misunderstandings, identity crises, fears, and stereotypes.

The book's goal is to help aspiring changemakers develop strategies for sustainable social-change projects. It serves as a guide for undergraduates, graduate students, and high-school upperclassmen in environmental studies, business, sociology, gender and sexuality, cross-cultural studies, music, religion, and communications and media.

Ann E. Feldman Ph.D. is a Visiting Scholar in Gender Studies and Sexuality at Northwestern University, USA, and Executive Director of the nonprofit Artistic Circles, USA.

T0323166

Routledge Focus on Media and Cultural Studies

Building Communities of Trust
Creative Work for Social Change

Ann E. Feldman

Routledge
Taylor & Francis Group

LONDON AND NEW YORK

First published 2022
by Routledge
4 Park Square, Milton Park, Abingdon, Oxon OX14 4RN

and by Routledge
605 Third Avenue, New York, NY 10158

*Routledge is an imprint of the Taylor & Francis Group, an informa
business*

© 2022 Artistic Circles

The right of Ann E. Feldman to be identified as author of this work
has been asserted in accordance with sections 77 and 78 of the
Copyright, Designs and Patents Act 1988.

Open Access publication of this title has been made possible via
generous funding from Artistic Circles, USA.

British Library Cataloguing-in-Publication Data
A catalogue record for this book is available from the British
Library

Library of Congress Cataloging-in-Publication Data
A catalog record for this book has been requested

ISBN: 978-1-032-25960-4 (hbk)
ISBN: 978-1-032-28349-4 (pbk)
ISBN: 978-1-003-29642-3 (ebk)

DOI: 10.4324/9781003296423

Typeset in Times New Roman
by Apex CoVantage, LLC

Contents

About the Author

Dr. Ann Feldman's career has been spent working with diverse communities around the world. Throughout her career, she has been motivated by curiosity and a deep desire to know other cultures, their needs and wants, and their values and fears.

The mission of Feldman's nonprofit Artistic Circles is to create collaborative media for social change and to build trust between varied communities. For the past 30 years, Dr. Feldman worked with partners in the US, Mexico, China, and India to produce internationally syndicated television and radio documentaries, public events, and musical CDs. Feldman showcased voices and faces seldom heard or seen in traditional media outlets. Her award-winning projects include *Water Pressures*, a partnership between desert villagers in Rajasthan, India, and the students and faculty at Northwestern University, (which is located on the shores of water-rich Lake Michigan in the US). *Water Pressures* was broadcast by American Public Television in the US, New Zealand, and Canada.

After 9/11, Feldman spent five years bringing together Chicago's Muslim, Jewish, and Christian communities in interfaith and diversity programs, which resulted in the *Ties That Bind* video documentary. The Emmy-nominated *Ties That Bind* premiered at the Council for the World's Parliament of Religions and UNESCO conference "Pathways to Peace" in Barcelona, Spain. It was syndicated nationally by the National Educational Telecommunications Association and internationally by John McLean Media.

Feldman also created radio documentaries focusing on women, music, and minorities, which were broadcast in the US on Public Radio International, WFMT public radio, and the WFMT Network. These included the *Unbreakable Spirits* series about women and girls in China; *Noteworthy Women* about women composers and scholars in the US and Mexico; and *Women at an Exposition* about the women leaders of the Chicago World's Fair of 1893.

Dr. Feldman is Visiting Scholar in Gender Studies and Sexuality at Northwestern University and Executive Director of the nonprofit Artistic Circles.

Figures

Acknowledgments

My deepest gratitude goes to the tens of thousands of people in the US, China, Mexico, and India who joined together into powerful communities of trust to create our media projects for social change. From beginning to end, this was a team effort.

My husband Mark has stood by my side for 32 years as we saw these projects come to life. Our family—Marc, Darleen, Sadie, Kaylin, David, Laura, Naomi, and Sammy—taught me how to laugh and trust myself. Julia Kramer was my intellectual sparring partner and an incomparable historian and researcher. Valerie Geller took precious time from her own media career to carefully and lovingly edit this book. Friends Hazel, Jessica, and Courtney believed in me when I doubted myself.

My Visiting Scholar appointment at Northwestern University's Department of Gender Studies and Sexuality gives me a home base and access to wonderful student interns, including Eliza, Emily, Meredith, Emily G, Sasha, Vlad, and Genevieve. Louise Neidorf and the Wilmette Public Library located important research for me, while the Special Collections at the University of Chicago Library has housed "Artistic Circles" archives and provided me with valuable documents.

Artistic Circles Board members supported our ground-breaking work, especially Deb McBride, Marge Graham, Carolyn Gifford, Andrea London, Potter Palmer, Kathy Flanagan, Katherine Bateman, and Kineret Jaffe. Funders critical to our success were The Illinois Humanities Council, Illinois Arts Council, Playboy Foundation, PepsiCo, Exelon, the Sehgal and Tata Foundations, IDCA, IBM, Sara Lee Foundation, and so many private contributors. Special thanks to WTTW and Marie Considine for shepherding our video documentaries to national syndication.

Early on, Routledge's editor Suzanne Richardson and Tanushree Baijal saw the value of this book, for which I am deeply grateful. Technical wizard Erik Gulbrandsen and copyeditor Sue Baugh finalized the book for publication.

Writer and philosopher Sachin Waikar, along with expert Carol Zsolnay, understood the value of adding case studies to inspire the next generation of leaders to create social change. Building communities of trust through arts and media is our shared legacy—one we need to pass on to future trust builders.

Introduction

Repair the World Through Trust: The Path to Social Impact

Change is possible when our hearts open to outsiders. People are often taught that they are better or worse than others. They're taught to hate or envy or ignore other communities. However, when individuals start questioning those beliefs, then honest dialogue opens and trust begins. Creative documentaries, public presentations, and the arts can expand those honest interactions. Trust begets trust.

The Challenge

Why we read this book?

Do You Have the Ideas and Passion to Build Your Own Social Justice Project?

- To make a difference
- To develop solutions
- To create a *better* world

Do You Want to Create a Social Change Project Using the Power of Media to Amplify Your Message?

This book can help you. Building Communities of Trust: *Creative Work for Social Change* offers the core lessons learned by thousands of participants in the US, China, Mexico, and India over a 30-year period. Together, we co-created social change documentaries for radio and TV, musical CDs, articles, books, concerts, town hall meetings, and college courses.

DOI: 10.4324/9781003296423-1

Trust is a key to creating positive social impact. Without trust, social change is unsustainable. And without media projects, the lessons learned remain within the small community of participants. Projects created for TV, radio, public programs, theater, concerts, musical CDs, books, and articles use creativity, artistry, and beauty to capture and share those messages with thousands, even millions of people worldwide. Trust and media can be powerful allies, but without trust, media can be inauthentic.

Trust is something earned. It can take a long time to build and can evaporate in a single ill-advised interaction. Sustaining commitments and connections is hard when individuals and communities that have joined together experience hardships, failures, and bumps in the road. This book is a roadmap of what my colleagues and I experienced together when creating collaborative media for social change. In this book, 40 of these colleagues share their wisdom about how to stay the course while overcoming all kinds of setbacks.

The first lesson we learned is: create powerful networks among diverse communities and within a variety of arts and media. How? Find the people who know people who know people. That's how we built communities of difference—participants from various countries, religions, gender identities, and economic and political situations joined together. Before your project goes public, first create within your group the change you want to see.

How Do You Recruit Others?

- **Identify those who share your passion.**
- **Bring together both the like-minded and those with opposing points of view—different races, ethnicities, and gender identities, who live all over the world.**
- **Connect your virtual community.**

Building communities of trust is a two-way street. In convincing people to give you their time, their knowledge, their expertise, and their money, they need to know that they can trust *you*. There are no shortcuts to this process.

The story of this book is about developing trust—where and how we succeeded and failed, the resilience we found amid failure to try again, and the hard knowledge we learned of when to walk away. Most of all, we relied on our partners to speak for themselves. By filming and recording their ideas and interactions, we shared their points of view with viewers and listeners on television and radio, and through musical CDs, books, articles, town hall meetings, and classroom discussions. *The key was to present everyone's authentic ideas, points of view, and disagreements, and to capture this through lasting creative products.*

In this book, you'll also hear the honest (and sometimes painful) feedback from more than 40 colleagues on projects we created *together*. There

Figure 0.1 Two male students from Chicago public high schools discussing their fears and stereotypes.

Source: Photograph by Nan Stein Photography LLC, reproduced with permission

were marvelous and harrowing adventures, we hugged and cursed each other, hit roadblocks, and then worked hard to find ways around them. In the end, new relationships worked, or they didn't, but we learned a great deal from trying.

Trust isn't often discussed in undergraduate and graduate classrooms, but the contributors to this book believe that the classroom—the incubator of future leaders—is the ideal environment to question, unpack, reassemble, and come up with new strategies for trust. All our partnerships were created through alliances with colleges and universities. The students' and faculties' creativity made the ideas come alive.

Here are the basic principles of TRUST and lists of undergraduate and graduate courses to target for the topic in each chapter.

Chapter 1: Shift From "Me" to "We"

Step away from self-reliance and join with others to create positive social change. Targeted courses are nonprofit management, religion and ethics, psychology, and behavioral science.

Chapter 2: Leaders and Role Models

Imitate models of partnerships rather than competition. Targeted courses are nonprofit management, leadership skills, gender and sexuality, public policy, and organizational behavior.

Chapter 3: Gender and Media—"Noteworthy Women"

Create win–win situations where showcasing the artistic achievements of culturally diverse individuals and groups fills a niche market for major media. Targeted courses are radio and TV, business management, marketing, gender studies and sexuality, and music.

Chapter 4: Control—China & "Unbreakable Spirits"

Protect the safety of all participants instead of seizing an opportunity for personal advancement. Targeted courses are Asian-American studies, international studies, music, radio and TV, journalism, and studies in gender and sexuality.

Chapter 5: Identity: "The Eternal Feminine"

Use the arts to build inclusiveness and conversations: for use in music composition, music performance, music history, interdisciplinary studies, gender studies and sexuality, marketing, and nonprofit management.

Chapter 6: Connect: "Ties That Bind"

In the aftermath tragedy or crisis, create peace projects that bring diverse communities together. Targeted courses are religion, ethics, Islamic studies, radio and TV, leadership skills, and gender studies and sexuality.

Chapter 7: Water Hierarchy: "Water Pressures"

Invite stakeholders from competing and opposing industries to the table to solve global problems. Targeted courses are environmental studies, earth sciences, engineering, film studies, infectious diseases, gender studies and sexuality, and MBA organizational management, leadership skills, and business strategies.

Chapter 8: Save Yourself: Trauma and Mindfulness

Learn to recognize when it's time to walk away from a social change project. Targeted courses are mental health, religion and ethics, international studies, and film studies.

Each chapter also presents case studies based on interviews of undergraduate and graduate students, who shared their own visions of how to build communities of trust, the hurdles, and strategies to achieve success. The case studies update the issues and voices of social change to help current students engage in the work of creatively building communities of trust. The studies were written by Sachin Waikar, Ph.D., with consultation by Carol Zsolnay.

Facing Your Fears About Trust

Venturing out of our comfort zones is awkward and scary. But before we can do authentic work with anyone who is different from us, we need to face our own fears.

The process starts by asking tough questions:

> What could happen in going forward? Could I become damaged or get hurt? Could I change so much that I'll alienate people I care about or lose important relationships with family and friends? Would people in these new communities resent, misunderstand, dislike, or maybe even hate me? Or ignore me?

As we began to know people who were different from us, we found comfort in their presence. These were people who had suffered, been resilient, and had successfully climbed some sort of mountain, for example, the first in the family to go to college, those who worked to help people in need, those who created spectacular art and music despite all odds, and who found the courage to speak their truth to power while creating beauty. People can use their "outsider" status and work to reach their potential and to become powerful "insiders."

And they're magnetic! These are people we want to be among and to be like, to introduce to others, showing how fascinating supposed "outsiders" really are. By knowing them, we *all* become better people.

To ignite a revolution of outsiders—to find and connect people who can work together to change the world in ways they choose—has been a driving goal of Artistic Circles for 30 years, and it continues today. We've learned to use the power of media and creativity to build programs that inspire and move others to work for social change.

And we want to show you how to do the same.

The World Has Cracked Open—The Time Is Now

The time is *now*. We are living through extraordinary global change. Climate disasters, COVID-19, gender and racial inequity, the brutal killing of African Americans, George Floyd and Breonna Taylor, and the peaceful/violent protests in response make this an anxious, stressful, and painful time. Many traditional symbols, old flags, and statues are coming down and tough conversations are happening.

Yet being very uncomfortable is an important part of the process of social change. On the cusp of terrible discomfort is where things really happen. *That's* when we leave the safety of the sameness and engage with people who are different—on *their* turf, in *their* environments, following *their* agendas, listening, and helping, because *that's* how real change works.

In all of this, no one is completely right or wrong. That's why there's a unique opportunity and need to create communities of trust right now. Our survival depends on it.

Since 1989, Artistic Circles' mission has been to try to make things right in an unfair world, or at try to least make things *better* for others—not in the way *we* think the solutions should advance, but rather by tuning in to what other communities need and want. We understand that the beauty and softness of the arts are ways to help different communities engage with each other and share their opinions. They know that once they are filmed or recorded, their words and actions will have an indelible stamp on the documentaries that can reach millions worldwide.

When looking back at 30 years of building communities of trust with media, we broke new ground and had great fun doing it. Every one of the eight media projects featured in this book was cutting-edge. We took lots of risks and crossed barriers of gender, race, religion, nationalities, identity, environmental stakeholders, and mental health.

Building Communities of Trust is part memoir, part template, and part storytelling. While these Artistic Circles' projects happened with me as the "face," they were never about me. This is about communities joining together to better their own lives. My story is woven within a much larger one, so that others, like you, can more easily navigate the minefields you'll face in working for change.

A friend and colleague put our work in perspective: "The irony is that the issues you addressed through your media programs have become *more timely* than when you created them 20 to 30 years ago."

The work of social justice is challenging and painful at times.

We learned that while we may not get it right all the time, we can live with ourselves because we tried. We learned to trust our sense of right and wrong.

You *will* make mistakes along the way. We did.

You'll often want to quit. But if you stick with it and find your way, meaningful results can happen.

You *can* change the world!

Don't Wait

- **Start now!**
- **If you have passion and great ideas, others will join you.**
- **Once you create Communities of Trust, magical things can happen.**

Figure 0.2 Students from Rajasthan, India, waving to visitors, and producer with video camera.

Source: Photograph by James Ward Ewing, reproduced with permission

1 Shift From "Me" to "We"

When You Lose It All, Find Your Destiny

> When your career, relationships, or health fall apart, that's the time to trust in your own resilience and follow your instincts. It's the time of great possibilities and an opportunity to join with others to initiate positive social impact. Through creative tools and the right partners, you can greatly expand your circles of influence.

When I lost my voice, I found my true destiny.

Literally.

As a professional singer, little things can wear you down—a bad review, a cracked high note, that scratchy tickle in your throat before a big performance, and even your own drive for perfection. There's a constant pressure on those invisible golden cords.

Most people don't know that vocal cords require constant care. You don't go out in the rain or cold. You go to sleep when you want to stay up late. You don't shout even when someone makes you angry, and instead of your favorite beverage, you ask for water. Every singer is vulnerable, from the greatest opera star to rock and pop stars Adele, Lady Gaga, Sam Smith, and Mariah Carey.

If your vocal cords get inflamed, damaged, or even worse—form nodes—you are **silenced**. We singers can be squashed so easily.

The Disaster

Singing was one of my greatest joys—a full-body experience of ecstasy that I shared with audiences. As a professional, I sang the lead in operas and performed as a soloist in recitals and in churches and synagogues.

DOI: 10.4324/9781003296423-2

Disaster struck when I was 38, at one of the biggest gigs of my professional singing career. I'd been hired as the cantorial soloist for a 2,500-member congregation for the Jewish High Holidays, a marathon filled with ten days of singing, often for six hours a day. No piano or organ—only me and the amateur choir.

I was so ready. I'd apprenticed to the best of the best—Cantor Abraham Lubin—and been a soloist for the great composer Max Janowski. However, I was nervous. This was a major opportunity and my first time as a cantorial soloist for such a huge synagogue during the Jewish High Holidays.

Right from the beginning, things started to go wrong. The rabbi was controlling, insisting that I learn 30 new pieces of music and perfect my Hebrew. During rehearsals, he picked at every little mistake. That did nothing to ease the pressure already on me to perform and sing beautifully.

I knew I had the ability, but I was also afraid. The responsibility of leading this congregation through prayerful song for these most sacred days of the year sat squarely on *my* shoulders.

The final straw came during the last week of rehearsals, when the rabbi insisted that I lie down and practice a full prostration on the *bima* (raised stage) for the *Hineni*, the holiest prayer:

> *Here I am*
> *I plead for mercy for myself*
> *And for those who have sent me.*

While most cantors just bow from the waist during this prayer, the rabbi directed me to lie face down on the floor, arms extended "like a cross." I'd worn a short dress that day, which hiked up each time I prostrated. He made me prostrate again and again. It was intimidating and not without sexual overtones. Finally, I'd had it. I stood up and shouted, "Enough!"

But inside me lurked the "good girl." What was the price for talking back to a religious leader?

The guilt went directly to my throat, a final indignity for my over-taxed vocal cords. I woke up the next morning with total laryngitis, unable even to speak, let along sing. This disaster hit four days before the High Holidays and the beginning of my big ten-day cantorial job.

I tried everything to relieve the symptoms, but the usual homeopathic remedies didn't work. On the suggestion of other singers, I went to see a famous throat specialist.

He sent me off with words of comfort and a prescription for Prednisone. I asked if it was safe to exert, even push my voice on these steroids. He assured me there was "no problem." He was wrong, but I wouldn't find out until later.

For those ten holy days, my voice soared. No phrase was too high or hard for me. I felt like Superwoman—I could do anything, sing anything, all while praying.

But as soon as I finished the course of steroids, I crashed. The let-down was like no other I've ever experienced. Even worse, within days I could barely speak. Forget singing. My larynx hurt every time I tried to talk.

According to a speech specialist I consulted, I had damaged the muscles around the vocal cords by pushing too hard while singing on steroids.

The cure was complete silence. I was not to use my voice in any way: "No singing, no talking, no whispering for a month." Back to pen and paper to communicate.

Lessons From Challenges

How could I stop everything? I had responsibilities—two daughters to raise, and commitments to fulfill, including several upcoming professional gigs.

But I followed orders. One month turned into three and then six.

It was brutal. In the silence, I felt like a caged lioness. My nickname as a child had been "Annie busy." I always needed to do something.

Yet during those silent months, I took a long, realistic look at my singing career. While it was my passion, I was already in my late 30s and hadn't yet built a national career, and now most likely never would. I'd been a good singer and excellent musician and combined my spirituality with vocal technique as a cantor.

However, as my speaking and singing voice came back bit by bit, both were limited. Some of the richness of my voice was still there but in a shorter, less usable vocal range. As I began to take serious stock of my life, my passion for singing waned.

Where was my place in the world now? What could I contribute? I sat mute as my kids flourished in school, and my husband expanded his law practice. I felt wrapped in a cocoon, letting the forces of my driving nature and current situation battle it out.

Maybe it took losing my singing voice to find my true one. I could feel myself changing into something. I just didn't know what. Inside, memories and emotions from the past kept surfacing, challenging everything I thought I knew.

Finding a Different Future

As I began to search for what was next, I tried to find models I could follow. Motivational books and inspirational biographies weren't much help. What finally turned the tide came from an unlikely source, a science project our seven-year-old daughter, Laura, brought home from school. For the project, each student was given a young caterpillar and a milkweed plant inside a handmade box.

Every day we watched that caterpillar gorge itself, until one day, it spun a cocoon and hung upside down in the box. The caterpillar was changing into a chrysalis.

I researched what happens to the chrysalis and discovered that from the beginning, a caterpillar contains all it needs to become a butterfly. But only in the cocoon can the change occur. I could relate to that. Looking deeply into my past, I re-imagined the use of my body, heart, and soul, just like that chrysalis.

I began to trust this strange and magical process within me. Unformed dreams of wanting to create social change through the arts and media started to emerge. What might my life and career be like if I channeled my enormous energy and diverse talents to helping others instead of being consumed by my singing ambitions?

At the same time, I was scared. Did I have the organizational skills and grit to create a life devoted to social change?

As the bits and pieces of my life floated up from the deep recesses of my memory, I recalled times when I was a leader, when I showed compassion, when I was responsible, and when I was an activist. I made a list, hoping a pattern might emerge, and relying on the process to lead me in the right direction.

My leadership came out when just 11. I won a music competition and played a Mozart piano concerto with adult professional musicians from the Chicago Symphony Orchestra. While still in high school, I taught Upward Bound students at a local college. During college, I helped others by setting up study sessions to prepare students for exams. And then, as an MA student at American University, I lectured full time at George Washington University, even though at age 22, I was younger than my graduate students.

During a challenging childhood, compassion came naturally to me. I learned to use music to soothe others through my piano-playing and singing. Compassion was also the basis for my singing as a professional. I found I was happiest as a soloist in church and temple.

Married at 21, I needed a steady singing gig instead of relying on occasional freelance pickup jobs. I found what looked like a stable job as a cantor and spent two years apprenticing to become a cantorial soloist, a career I hoped would last until well into my 60s. During that time, I also completed my Ph.D. in the History of Culture from the University of Chicago.

But in my early 30s, something changed. I became aware of the injustices of the world, especially for women in the arts. I was excited by the music of women composers and began singing concerts that often premiered their new compositions. I joined a Women Cantors Network and spoke up at national conferences on behalf of women's ordination as cantors for Jewish synagogues.

Five years later, leadership, compassion, responsibility, and activism all converged in a single project. I produced the first recording of music by Guggenheim-winning composer Ruth Crawford Seeger, not just her contemporary music but also her folk songs and blues. I raised the funds, hired musicians from the Chicago Symphony, managed the sessions, helped edit and produce the recording, and found a record company to distribute it.[1]

At the age of 38, with a rapidly waning singer career, could I parlay music and media production into a future career? Friends, colleagues, advisors, professionals, funders, and even former doubters all said, "Yes."

With help from attorney Linda Thoren Neal, I formed and filed for a 501(c)(3) nonprofit, which could accept donations and not have to pay taxes. Of course, a nonprofit needs a board of directors, so I invited artist female friends and academic colleagues to join us.

We called our new nonprofit Artistic Circles to show our focus on the arts and the interconnectedness of arts, history, literature, science, politics, and advocacy. We were a hodge-podge group, many of us never having sat on a board of directors (including me), but we all shared the same passion and mission: "To discover and present the artistic achievements and stories of culturally diverse women."

This path felt true to me—this was my higher calling, my destiny. The caterpillar was beginning to transform from a chrysalis into a butterfly. We could do this!

"We" Instead of "Me"

My biggest challenge along the way was learning to trust others. I'd been self-reliant from an early age and learned that the solo path was safer and more dependable than leaning on others. But social change is not a job for a soloist—it's a team effort.

When I lost my voice, I learned a big life lesson—to focus on "we" instead of "me." I saw that not only could I trust myself to follow a new career, but I could also rely on others to co-create the social changes we wanted to see in the world.

Chapter 1 Case Study: Learning the Business of Music

Maria and Grier were unsure of the best way forward.

Maria, a soprano, and Grier, a cellist, had been performing musical pieces together, from classical to contemporary, for several years. Each also had an international career in partnership with other musicians.

Now, in the fall of 2020, they had come up with an exciting idea. They wanted to produce a CD of previously unrecorded music by living composers from the US, the Netherlands, Germany, and South Africa. "We saw the work as an important contribution to the global music repertoire, one that would publicize living composers worldwide, including well-known and lesser-known ones."

Maria and Grier had to think carefully about the next steps. Raising the required funds for recording the CD—an estimated $15,000—would have been challenging under any circumstances. However, the COVID-19 pandemic was in full force, changing the face of collaboration in every way.

For starters, audio engineers, editors, and other sound technicians were wary about working in a confined space, especially with an unmasked singer, during the pandemic. Also, few recording venues remained open for business at the time. In addition, not many prospective funders in the duo's network and beyond were willing to meet face to face. Finally, neither Grier nor Marie had any experience developing a business plan or fundraising for the project. "This is all new to us," Grier said, "but we're willing to learn what's needed about the business of music to succeed with our CD."

The Business of Music: Key Considerations

As they began researching the business of music, Marie and Grier broke the subject into several categories:

Opportunity cost: A friend with a business background told them to consider "opportunity cost" carefully. What would they be giving up to produce the CD? Was it worth the time, financial cost, and effort they would have to put into it? They also had to recognize that due to the pandemic, live performance opportunities were rare.

Financial costs: The musicians didn't know what their total cost of creating and marketing the CD might be. A contractor who had produced a similar-length CD said, "Expect to spend about $15,000." But would their needs be similar to that artist's? They tried to estimate their cost components, including audio engineering, production of CD copies, distribution, marketing, legal, and other expenses. They also thought about how they might reduce costs, perhaps making their work available through streaming services along with or even instead of a physical CD.

Market factors: As they learned more, the pair realized that they hadn't considered the market, or target audience, they were trying to serve: people with an interest in classical music, especially those who might buy recordings of previously unreleased tracks rather than popular "classics." How large was the audience in their target markets, the US and Europe? What were those people willing to spend?

Nor had they thoroughly considered the competition. Were there other CDs or streaming offerings out there competing for the same audiences?

Funding sources: If Marie and Grier remained confident about their CD product after doing some of the analyses, they still had to think about raising funds. Their personal network was the most logical place to start, but they had to determine whom to approach and how. There were also newer crowdsourcing options such as Kickstarter and Fractured Atlas. How could they decide among these? What effort would it require to approach the different sources? How should they position themselves when asking for funding? Should they follow a script that explained their "ask" and why the potential funder should invest? If so, what would that script contain?

Collaborators: As noted earlier, a major challenge Maria and Grier faced was finding venues, audio engineers, and editors willing to work with them during the COVID-19 pandemic, when most collaborators were avoiding the in-person contact that music recording required. They had to locate the right team who believed in their product and could be trusted to deliver high-quality work at an affordable price. Then, they had to find the right record company to distribute their music, or consider doing it themselves, including all the marketing.

Legal: The duo also realized that they hadn't considered all the legal issues involved in creating a CD, such as securing rights from the composers, agreements between themselves and with the recording and editing crew, and rights to images and text for the CD booklet.

Roles: Finally, the artists had to decide what their individual roles for the project would be. Who would do what, in terms of developing the business idea further and approaching and following up with prospective funding sources? Their roles in composing and performing music had been clear and straightforward. Now, they had to consider how to divide their labor for their new, business-focused collaboration.

Questions to Consider

Put yourself in Maria and Grier's place and think about their challenges. How you would answer the following questions?

1.   How would you determine opportunity and financial costs? How would you decide whether to pursue the project in the first place?
     Do some online research to develop a line-item budget based on estimated costs for a CD project like this. How close to the $15,000 is it? Why might your estimate be significantly lower or higher?

2. What market factors should Marie and Grier take into account? Again, do brief online research to understand current purchasing trends related to classical music and the potential competition the two musicians might face. How would these factors affect this project?
3. What funding sources for the project are worth considering? How would you decide which to prioritize over others, including online crowdsourcing options? What kind of funding script do you think would work best? How would you prepare to pitch your project to prospective investors on both intellectual and emotional levels?
4. How would you find collaborators, especially given the constraints of the pandemic? What questions would you ask potential collaborators to determine their qualifications and compatibility as partners?
5. What legal issues do the musicians need to address for the CD, such as securing rights and other contracted terms? What's the best way to go about deciding what legal help to enlist?
6. How do you think the roles should be split between Grier and Marie for this project? Should they share all responsibilities 50–50 or assign specific tasks to one another? What are the pros and cons of each approach?
7. How can they find a record company whose interests match the content and quality of the CD? What factors should they consider in negotiating a contract? What additional marketing can they do to help promote international sales? What are the potential costs of that marketing? Can they go back to their initial funders for more support, if needed?

Note

1 *Music of Ruth Crawford Seeger*. Musical Heritage Society, 1988. LP release. MHS 9122292.

References

1. Brown, Brene. *Dare to Lead: Brave Work, Tough Conversations, Whole Hearts.* New York: Random House, 2018.
2. Block, Stephen R. *Why Nonprofits Fail: Overcoming Founder's Syndrome, Fundphobia and Other Obstacles to Success.* San Francisco: Jossey-Bass, 2003.
3. Christfort, Kim and Suzanne Vickberg. *Business Chemistry: Practical Magic for Crafting Powerful Work Relations.* Hoboken, NJ: Wiley, 2018.
4. Counts, Alex. *Changing the World Without Losing Your Mind: Lessons from Three Decades of Social Entrepreneurship.* Pittsburgh: Rivertown Books, 2019.
5. Jackson, Phil and Hugh Delehanty. *Eleven Rings: The Soul of Success.* New York: Penguin Press, 2013.

2   Leaders and Role Models

Chicago World's Fair Women:
Look to Women of the Past to
Show Us How to Lead in the
Present

When you don't have a mentor, can't trust current leaders, or you don't "see yourself" in the leaders around you, you can search for mentors in the past. Those models of choice—in our case, women leaders from Chicago's 1893 World's Fair—can teach you how to build communities of trust across the boundaries of nationality, class, race, education, economics, and worldview. They can show you models of partnerships to create and lead social-change organizations. You can then use the power of theater, music, and public programs to widely disseminate your social impact messages.

Inspired by the women leaders of the 1893 World's Fair in Chicago, Artistic Circles created art, music, theater, and media projects for the Fair's Centenary in 1993. These projects included the Grammy-nominated musical CD, *Women at an Exposition*; the gold medal-winning radio program, *Politics and Old Lace*; and the Benjamin Franklin's award-winning book, *World's Fair Notes*.

Motivation to Tell "Herstory"

Throughout my three undergraduate and graduate degrees, my coursework never included a piece of music by a woman composer nor musicology texts by women. At the time, I didn't question my teachers about this omission, but by my late 30s, I woke up to this dissonance. There was a whole world of music, arts, history, and accomplishments by women leaders, which fascinated me. By the time I turned 40, I needed to find my own way of discovering and presenting "Herstory."

DOI: 10.4324/9781003296423-3

Our board of directors for Artistic Circles agreed on a common mission: "To discover and present the artistic achievements and stories of culturally diverse women." We were motivated to make our first mark by telling Herstory, but what would be our vehicle?

I discovered our first project when an art history expert handed me a brochure calling for submissions for the 1993 centenary celebrations of the 1893 Chicago World's Fair. While the brochure lauded the achievements of the city of Chicago in hosting an international fair, there was no mention of the women leaders.

I found that jarring, since I knew about the ground-breaking Woman's Building and Women's Educational Congresses. Since 1985, I'd scoured libraries, private collections, and the scholarly network for histories of those women, focusing on music composed and performed by women. I sang at concerts, gave presentations, and wrote an article for Harvard's *NOTES* about women's music at the World's Fair.[1]

As a cultural historian and budding feminist, that exclusion of the World's Fair women rankled and intrigued me. Maybe that was *our* story to tell—a niche our nonprofit could fill. My artistic instincts went on high alert.

Rediscovering the Pillars of Herstory

By digging through library archives, I discovered that there were two pillars of women's representation at the 1893 World's Fair. One was the impressive 388 x 199 foot Woman's Building, and the other was the Women's Educational Congresses presented at Chicago's Art Institute over six months. With 27,000,000 national and international visitors to the World's Fair, women had an unprecedented platform to highlight their ideas, accomplishments, and social/political demands. It was ground-breaking for the Fair to bring together diverse women leaders of the day—suffragist Susan B. Anthony, race activist Ida B. Wells, settlement leader Jane Addams, adventuress/reporter Nellie Bly, as well as temperance leaders, economic and educational specialists, and traditional homemakers.

I wondered why their history was generally unknown and why those stellar models from the past weren't imitated and expanded in the present.

We decided to take that model from the past and use it to create communities of trust in 1993.

Bertha and Ellen: Women Leaders of the World's Fair

The two major stages for women's representation at the Fair were managed by upper class women, Bertha Palmer and Ellen Henrotin. While their worldviews and governing styles were quite different, they trusted one another. They used their complementary talents and networks to manage their separate fiefdoms at the World's Fair—the Woman's Building for Bertha and the Women's Educational Congresses for Ellen.

Bertha Palmer was president of the Board of Lady Managers at the World's Fair. Through her husband and his powerful friends on the Board of Directors of the Fair, she lobbied the US government to pay $200,000 for a Woman's Building. Despite opposition from the men, she hired the first female architect in America to design the neoclassical building. And, through her personal connections with European royalty, she assembled a collection of women's arts and handicrafts from around the world.

Ellen Henrotin ran the Women's Congress Auxiliary. Instead of displaying arts and crafts and material goods, she focused on ideas, many of them radical for the day. She brought in speakers to challenge the status quo, such as suffragist Susan B. Anthony, who demanded the vote for women; Fannie Barrier Williams, who fought for jobs for African-American women; and women of the press who wanted their own voices and stories heard in the newspapers of the day.

Bertha Palmer sought to display women's power, especially through a separate building and through the arts. She spoke at the opening of the Fair:

> Official representation for women upon so important an occasion as the present, is unprecedented. It is official, acting under government authority and sustained by government funds. Even more important than the discovery of Columbus, which we are gathered together to celebrate, is the fact that the general Government has just discovered woman.[2]

Ellen Henrotin was a pragmatist. Married to the founder and director of the Chicago Stock Exchange, she knew that money was power.

> There is no more patent sign of the times than the fact that woman is attracting the attention of the financial world, and that her large property interests are being recognized as an integral part of the so-called "Woman Question." The keynote of the relation of the sexes is really a financial one.[3]

Bertha and Ellen worked closely as partners. To better understand the vast accomplishments of the Woman's Building and Women's Educational Congresses, I also needed a partner—an historian to research the original source material buried in old newspapers, minutes of the Board of Lady Managers, speeches of the day, albums of women's clubs, old photographs, and wax cylinder recordings, while I built public programs.

A Model for Partnership From the Past

Through a colleague, I learned about Julia Wood Kramer, an historian and researcher who knew about the World's Fair, especially the female reformers. Julia was a feminist with an impressive business background. In 1949, she had graduated from the Harvard Radcliffe Program in Business Administration—an achievement rare for women at that time. She was able to put Ellen Henrotin and the feminists at the Educational Congresses into historical context. Her impeccable research and constant questioning of historical "givens" cemented our relationship.

Julia was my opposite—a tall, White Anglo-Saxon Protestant whose family came over on the *Mayflower*. I was a little scrappy Jewish girl from Indiana. As we got to know each other, we took long walks and talked and argued about the World's Fair women who had invaded our lives.

Julia, impatient with the incomplete and inaccurate "handed-down stories" of the World's Fair women, went to the chatty 19th-century newspapers, which told more of the story and added descriptions of the juicy parts of the Fair. She learned that there had been a scandal and a lawsuit against Bertha Palmer, the socialite president of the Board of Lady Managers of the

Figure 2.1 The author with researcher Julia Kramer.

Source: Photograph by the author

Woman's Building. Also, Palmer and her ladies had tried to keep out the suffragists and women of color.[4] But it was the suffragists and the African-American women who held the center stage at the Women's Educational Congresses at the Art Institute.

The research brought us back again and again to Bertha and Ellen, who had vastly different leadership styles. Bertha, as the president of the Board of Lady Managers, ran the organization and Woman's Building with an iron fist in a velvet glove. Her style was hierarchical, based on a male model of leadership. The Woman's Building was a major achievement for women—but only for upper-class White women.

Ellen's governance was more equitable. She saw her role as part of a larger movement for all women:

> This is a peaceful revolution in the social, legal, and moral status of women. Is there any abuse in the body politic to be reformed? At once a society is organized which arouses and educates public opinion on that subject. . . . It is the associate mind, the many hearts beating as one, that now move the world.[5]

That was a light bulb moment for me. Those polar opposites—Bertha Palmer and Ellen Henrotin, Woman's Building versus Women's Educational Congresses, homespun versus activist feminism—successfully worked together. That partnership could be the model and foundation on which our nonprofit would build our World's Fair projects.

Re-Purposing the Past to Guide Us in the Present

Artistic Circles was a lean nonprofit with no frills, which centered its activities on programming rather than structure. We modelled ourselves on Ellen Henrotin's "power of associations." While our female board was excited about showcasing the World's Fair women, potential partners and funders asked: "What do a Woman's Building and Educational Congresses from 100 years ago have to do with 1993?"

My answer: Many of the same problems women faced then still exist today. In 1893, activist Ida B. Wells railed against the exclusion of Black Americans from the Fair.[6] In 1992, in Los Angeles, there were bloody riots protesting the acquittal of four White policemen for the beating of Black motorist Rodney King. In the 1890s, women fought for the vote and equal pay. In the 1990s, women were still fighting the "glass ceiling" and trying to get ratification of the ERA (Equal Rights Amendment). While there have been advances for women and people of color, roadblocks to equity remain.

I decided to transform the 1893 leaders' stories that Julia discovered and create artistic programs to excite modern-day audiences.

Our first World's Fair project was a five-minute video demo showing the Woman's Building and featuring background music by women composers. That's when we faced our first roadblock. While we tried to raise the money to create a full-length documentary, we knew too little about how to attract big funding.

We backtracked from dreams of an hour-long video documentary to live, less-expensive projects. We created one-hour plays featuring the leading World's Fair women, not only Bertha Palmer, Ellen Henrotin, Susan B. Anthony, and Ida B. Wells, but also composer Amy Beach, women's rights activist Fannie Barrier Williams, painter Mary Cassatt, and reporter Nellie Bly. Actors portrayed the leaders, while musicians performed music written by women composers for the Fair.

Trust and Crossing the Gender Barrier

But there was still something missing in these stories—the human side of the World's Fair women. I contacted their descendants, found through personal interviews, letters, and documents, to see how they viewed their famous ancestors. Despite our research, the prominent leader Bertha Palmer remained as elusive and unapproachable as an icon.

That's when I found the courage to call the office of Potter Palmer IV, the great-great grandson of Bertha Palmer. Potter agreed to meet with me and told me that in addition to her remarkable leadership qualities, Bertha and her husband Potter were major art collectors and patrons. For the Woman's Building, Bertha commissioned artist Mary Cassatt to paint an enormous mural. Potter IV also revealed that the family called Bertha a real "stem-winder," meaning that she took risks and fought for what she believed in, even when it was unpopular within her own class.

With Potter's help, we were able to partner with major Chicago institutions. He introduced us to the management at the Chicago History Museum, who agreed to host our musical theater show about the World's Fair women. I was also invited to lecture at the prestigious Fortnightly Club, which had been founded by several women of the Fair, including Bertha Palmer. Potter joined Artistic Circles' board of directors, sharing with us the business knowledge he had developed over decades of managing companies.

Financial Credibility and the Media

We knew that our nonprofit organization needed serious funds to carry out its mission and to finance our projects. With Potter IV by my side, we visited foundations, government offices, and individuals to gain financial support. Potter recalls, "We had meetings, we'd go pound on doors and hope something happened. That's what was special – putting leather to the pavement. I was walking around doing something right."[7]

Eventually, we started to receive national funding. The Smithsonian Institution gave me a grant to do primary research at the Library of Congress. During that Fellowship, I befriended two female museum directors—Edie Mayo (American History) and Carolyn Carr (National Portrait Gallery). Together, we created a plan for a national partnership of current women leaders who were specialists on the World's Fair women.

We decided to recreate the 1893 Educational Congresses in 1993 by inviting leading female historians to Chicago for a gathering that we called "The Power of Associations Conference."

The strongest experience of that conference was the palpable sense of connection that the historians felt for their subjects of a century earlier, calling them "Sisters Across Time." The gathering also created a magical sense of sisterhood among the scholars and with us. Instead of competing, these women historians formed alliances.

Now, we needed a media project to "show, not tell" audiences about the beauty and talents of those World's Fair Women. We transformed the crumbling sheet music of the 1890s into a musical CD, which included parlor songs and violin and piano pieces by female composers. Most of that music hadn't been heard since the 1890s.

We attracted major talent for our recording—two internationally known singers (Susanne Mentzer and Sunny Joy Langton), a leading pianist (Kimberly Schmidt) and superb violinist (Elaine Skorodin), and one of the best audio engineers in the nation (Larry Rock). We called the recording *Women at an Exposition.*

Once we had a completed master, I pitched the recording to a dozen record companies. KOCH International picked it up, and when the CD was released in 1992, the first run of 2,500 copies sold out. Decades later, the CD is still available.[8] In 1992, *Women at an Exposition* was nominated for a Grammy award.

The CD brought Artistic Circles national recognition. We now had a calling card to convince others to collaborate with us on future projects. Every time Potter and I went to meet with a potential funder or partner, we'd gift them the CD, which showcased our ability to follow through and succeed with our projects.

Building Trust With Media and Government

We didn't only focus on music but also explored the media and politics. Julia Kramer discovered an entire congress at the 1893 World's Fair devoted to "Women and the Press." It was attended by reporters, editors, and press owners from the US, London, Stockholm, France, Canada, and Japan. That 1893 conference highlighted the communities of trust built *between* prominent press leaders and their organizations, dramatized by a "handshake" between the WCTU *Union Signal's* editor and Susan B. Anthony. That gesture indicated the Women Christian Temperance Union's public support of suffrage.[9]

Julia found the speeches of Susan B. Anthony, which demanded that women "get out the vote," and a pamphlet written by reporter Ida B. Wells, "The Reason Why the Colored American is Not in the World's Columbian Exposition." While Wells was excluded from the Woman's Building and Women's Congresses, she partnered with Frederick Douglass to create and disseminate her pamphlet to 10,000 visitors in the Haitian Building. That pamphlet told of the achievements of African Americans and the horrors of lynching.

By 1993, women had become a force in the media as editors, newspaper owners, and reporters, and made up more than a third of the staff in daily newspapers. We realized that between 1893 and 1993, newspapers had been a common denominator for women in media. How could we link media from the past to the present? Was it possible to create an event that looked backward and forward to today's women in the press?

The answer came from a surprising source—Chicago's Department of Cultural Affairs. Director Lois Weisberg was a close colleague of Mayor Daley and a cultural powerhouse in her own right who could create links with media, history, and audiences.[10]

Organizing the "Women and the Press"

When we proposed a conference, "Women and the Press: 1893 and 1993," Lois not only agreed to host it at the Chicago Cultural Center but also paid for CBS war correspondent Georgie Anne Geyer to come to Chicago. Newspapers usually competed for readers and awards, but various publications eagerly sent their reporters and editors to our conference. They included the editor-in-chief of *La Raza*, Chicago's leading Hispanic paper; race reporters from the *Guardian*; and disabilities and school reform reporters and editors from the *Chicago Tribune*. These editors and reporters showed us how many of the issues that women faced in the 1890s were still valid a century later. As I wrote:

> Women showed courage in dealing with sexual harassment, racial inequity, and advancing causes of interest to women and minorities in the news.[11]

The conference led to an invitation from Leo Harris, an editor of Pogo Press, for me to write a chapter called "Women and the Press from the 1893 Fair" for the book *World's Fair Notes* about women journalists at the Fair.

Reporter Georgie Anne Geyer wrote the preface to the book. *World's Fair Notes* won a Benjamin Franklin Award. Artistic Circles now had a CD and a chapter in an award-winning book as our national products.

Where and Why We Failed

Despite our successes, two of Artistic Circles' projects failed, one due to broken trust and another due to our own shortcomings. We recovered one project but not the other.

The one that failed completely was a book manuscript titled *The Power of Associations: A Documentary History of Women's Participation in the World's Columbian Exposition of 1893*. It represented eight years of research that Julia and I had conducted, gathering hundreds of forgotten primary and secondary sources written by and about the World's Fair women. These sources included their letters, photographs, documents, newspaper articles, unpublished speeches about women's use of public space, views of womanhood, women's exercise of power and philanthropy, and women's rights.

For two years, we worked with a major university press for the book's publication. Even though we had built trust with the editorial staff, they couldn't seem to make up their minds. Finally, they brought in a female historian, who advised them against publishing our manuscript. Julia and I believed that the historian had a competing agenda for her own work.

Our trust with the publisher was broken, which showed us that not all trust communities succeed. The experience remains a disappointment because of the inherent value of the material we gathered. However, as in the case of all failures, we needed to move on.

Another project failed due to our own shortcomings. Artistic Circles had developed our first full-length musical theater production about the World's Fair women. Even though the production had all the right ingredients, it still fell flat. The script played "softball" on difficult, unresolved issues of gender, race, and class inequity and disappointed our audiences and funders.

Creating a Show With Teeth

We vowed to recover this project. We asked professionals to take over and create a musical theater show with more controversy and drama. Playwrights and directors Kathleen Thompson and Michael Novak fit the bill. They owned a small theater company and had written scripts for decades. I challenged them to make the 1890s struggles for voting rights and for racial and gender equity come to life and inspire men and women in the 1990s.

The resulting theater production, *Politics and Old Lace*, dovetailed perfectly with an upcoming conference to be held at the University of Chicago,

"American Women in Higher Education" conference. What better place to engage modern women leaders with the stories of the 1890s women, on whose shoulders they stood?

Julia Kramer and I pitched this show to people she knew on the Women's Board at University of Chicago. We were gratified when they not only funded us but also gave us marching orders: "Help women of today gain strength from voices of the past." Once again, we were in our wheelhouse where our ideas and aspirations matched those of our partners.

The result: an original musical theater production filled with drama, conflicts, pathos, and inspiration. The opening scene was a tableau of the main World's Fair women, based on the long-lost mural that Mary Cassatt had painted for the World's Fair. As each of the female giants of the past came to life one by one, I was moved to tears. And when Fannie Barrier Williams gave her impassioned speech for equal rights for African Americans, there wasn't a dry eye in the house:

> Our women ask for the same opportunity for the acquisition of all kinds of knowledge that may be accorded to other women. Except teaching in colored schools and menial work, colored women can find no employment in this free America. Refusal of such employment because of color belies every maxim of justice and fair play.[12]

The audience erupted into applause after this speech. One of the attendees was WFMT radio's Lois Baum, a soft-spoken, elegant woman who worked as an associate producer at this classical radio station.

She approached me afterward and told me she loved the show. I could sense the steel in her backbone as we talked about how we could transform live theater into a radio broadcast. Lois, writer Michael Novak, and I reworked the script over and over. Lois constantly helped us match the power of our theatrical ardor with the possibilities and capabilities of radio. As she told me later:

> It was a breath of fresh air in my world to have you come in and have ideas and the energy and enthusiasm to see them through. That was a big thing for me. My own world was very carefully cut out with specific things I had to do each week, too many of them.[13]

Together, we transformed lost history into a vibrant radio program for national audiences. WFMT's syndication of *Politics and Old Lace* reached tens of thousands of listeners across the nation. Our heroes, past and present, went out on the airways, inspiring others to follow their lead. This production won the Gold Medal at the 1993 New York Broadcasting Festival. Artistic Circles now had its third media project.

Figure 2.2 Screenshot of actor Tina Marie Wright playing the role of African-American leader Fannie Barrier Williams from *Politics and Old Lace*.

Source: Photograph by the author

Context: Support = Social Change

The deeper we plunged into our projects, the clearer the message across the ages became: when women work together (often with support from men) and not separately, positive social change happens.

- By 1893, women had gained some property rights and were involved in municipal structural improvement, advances in higher education, and efforts to achieve voting rights.
- By 1993, women could vote and were pushing for reproduction rights, employment equality, and ratification of the Equal Rights Amendment (ERA).
- By 2021, women had made strides in Congress, had better pay equity (80% of what men made for the same work), and had an African-East-Indian-American Vice President, Kamala Harris.

- Still to achieve: universal childcare, equal representation in upper management and politics, an end to institutional racism and sexism, equity for people of color (Black Lives Matter), and freedom from sexual harassment (#MeToo movement).

Chicago's 1893 World's Fair was the template for women's cooperation that Artistic Circles brought to audiences across the nation. Through these programs, audiences learned from Herstory and gained understanding of many bigger issues: from the physical use of space at home and in the workplace; varied views of womanhood from traditionalists to activists; women's strategies to exercise power; to the conflicts that occurred (and still occur) over class, race, and economics.

The World's Fair women projects helped Artistic Circles stake its claim as a creator of collaborative media for social change—discovering a wrong that needed righting—along with a set of lessons that could help overcome current problems.

Today's emerging leaders can still mine the truths, lessons, and failures of past leaders to create their own social impact alliances and projects.

Chapter 2 Case Study: Finding the Right Professional Path and Role Models

Francoise Barry Nkosi needed guidance.

"FB," as he called himself, was Black and a South African native who had immigrated to the US with his parents when he was in middle school. Navigating the new culture was challenging at first, but FB made good progress with the help of mentors, including a Black middle-school teacher and others. "They really helped make me who I am today," he said.

After doing well as an engineering major in college, FB joined a technology consulting firm, where he had made consistently strong contributions. But recently he had been passed over for a promotion that he was well-qualified for, forcing him think about the systemic bias he faced and how to overcome it, hopefully with the help of mentors.

Early Life, Early Role Model

FB was born in Johannesburg, South Africa, to a South African father and a light-skinned French mother. Since his parents both worked for the American Embassy, he was sent to a primarily White school, with minimal exposure to Black students, teachers, or administrators.

In fact, the first time he had a Black teacher was when he was in the seventh grade and his family moved to Washington, DC.

> I met Ms. Casey, my English teacher, at a really pivotal time in my life. I didn't fit in. I wasn't Black enough for my Black peers or White enough for White peers. I spoke differently, had a funny accent, and didn't play basketball, even though I was tall and Black! But Ms. Casey believed in me and changed my life.

She helped the young FB navigate American culture as an outsider. "She was like a third parent who was really there for me," FB said.

Organizational Culture in Context

Skilled in math and science from an early age, FB had majored in electrical engineering in college and then joined a technology consulting firm. "My job was to find and fix engineering weaknesses in large companies, with a focus on electronic manufacturers," FB said. He had recently begun a part-time MBA at a prestigious business school.

However, FB's true passion was analyzing diversity in the context of majority systems and how the associated dynamics affected productivity and morale in the workplace. As a member of the Black minority in corporations, he had trouble trusting the White majority:

> I've felt like in some of the White spaces, I'm constantly on guard, always thinking about how I come off – too aggressive, threatening? Even though those are qualities often seen as strengths or at least respected in White colleagues. It was funny when the pandemic hit, and they're talking about keeping a six-foot distance from others, and I've been walking six feet away from people my whole life, to err on the safe side. That's nothing new to me.

In this context, FB used his analytical skills to consider cultural challenges he faced as a Black professional in a predominantly White organization. "I'm an engineer," he said.

> So, I think about organizational culture as an "input-output" thing. If you put something into the machine – the "black box" that is our culture – it will come out a certain way because it is built to make things that way. Until we change the black box, until we change the system in which we're operating, regardless of what you put in, it will make the same output because that's how it's built.

The Challenge of Professional Advancement

FB had to draw on that perspective when he faced a significant challenge at work. After nearly five years at his company, FB was passed up for a significant promotion in favor of a White candidate with lesser qualifications and experience:

> It felt unfair, but not that far off from what I expected. I've been passed over for lots of things in life, but this time I thought it might be different given how much I've proven myself. But it wasn't.

He noted that the development made sense in context, because he simply wasn't part of the dominant social structure at the company: "Everyone is friendly. But my White colleagues hang out a lot more with each other than anyone else – from the senior executives to the interns." Similarly, he struggled to find mentors in the organization, but eventually connected with Davis, a Black director-level executive who worked in a different practice within the firm.

Unsure of what to do next, FB asked Davis for advice. "He told me he understood that what had happened wasn't right," FB said.

> But we both knew there wasn't much he could do about it. He did offer to have me transferred to his division, where the hiring manager is also Black. He told me I'd have better access to training and new opportunities there, because he could help me out. But that felt kind of like accepting defeat – and why should I have to relocate because the system is flawed?

Frustrated but committed to finding a way forward, FB considered his next steps.

Questions to Consider

Put yourself in FB's shoes as you think about the following questions.

1. What are the racial, cultural, and other factors and dynamics at play in FB's professional situation?
2. How would you describe the social and organizational system FB is part of? What are its advantages and disadvantages for different demographic groups, including those from majority and minority culture? What do you think of FB's "black box" analogy for the cultural system. What is a real-life example you've seen of that system in action?
3. If you were in FB's place, what steps might you take to advance within the organization without compromising your ideals? How might you find

people to trust and potential allies and mentors? Would you consider transferring to work under the Black mentor and manager—why or why not?

4. How might you think beyond individual advancement, such as supporting junior colleagues from minority backgrounds? What mentorship and/or networking guidance could you provide?

5. Now, consider your own personal or professional situation as you answer the following questions:

- What systems do you inhabit that might include bias related to you or others? What's the nature of the bias and its potential sources?
- What challenges do the system present based on race or other demographics? What's the source of these challenges?
- What strategies could be used within a biased system to build communities of trust and find the right role models and mentors?
- Think about your own mentorship experiences. Have you benefited from mentors in your life? Who were they, and what did they do that was helpful? Have you mentored others? How do you help them navigate potentially biased systems and other challenges?

Notes

1 Ann Feldman. "Being Heard: Women Composers and Patrons at the 1893 World's Columbia Exposition," *Notes*, Second Series, September 1990, Vol. 47, No. 1, 7–20. Published by *Music Library Association Stable*, www.jstor.org/stable/940531.

2 Mrs. Potter Palmer. "Works of the Lady Managers," a speech given at the Opening Ceremonies of the World's Columbian Exposition in May 1893. Published as *Dedication and Opening Ceremonies of the World's Columbian Exposition* (Chicago: A.L. Stone, 1891).

3 Ellen Martin Henrotin. "The Financial Independence of Women," in: Mary Kavanaugh Oldham, ed., *The Congress of Women: World's Columbian Exposition, Chicago U. S.A., 1893* (Chicago: Monarch Book Company, 1894), 348.

4 Julia Kramer, in an email to Ann Feldman, March 16, 2019.

5 Henrotin, op.cit.

6 Ida B. Wells, ed., *The Reason Why the Colored American Is Not in the World's Columbian Exposition*, 1893, https://digital.library.upenn.edu/women/wells/exposition/exposition.html.

7 Potter Palmer, in an interview with Ann Feldman, December 5, 2018.

8 Link to *Women at an Exposition*, https://amazon.com/Women-Exposition-Composed-Performed-Chicgo/dp/B000001SH8.

9 Ann Feldman. "Women and the Press," in: *World's Fair Notes* (Minneapolis: Pogo Press, 1893), 94.

10 Malcom Gladwell. "Six Degrees of Lois Weisberg," *The New Yorker*, January 3, 1999, Archives, p. 52.

11 Ann Feldman, personal Day-timers Journal, August 18, 1993.

12 Fannie Barrier Williams. "The Intellectual Progress of the Colored Women of the United States Since the Emancipation Proclamation," in: Mary K.O. Eagle,

ed., *The Congress of Women, Held in the Woman's Building* (Chicago: Monarch Book Company, 1893), 696–711.

13 Lois Baum, in an interview with Ann Feldman, December 3, 2018.

References

1. Feldman, Ann E. and Julia W. Kramer, eds. *The Power of Associations: A Documentary History of Women's Participation in the World's Columbian Exposition of 1893*. Includes hundreds of primary and secondary sources written by and about the women at the World's Fair, Unpublished manuscript, 1992.
2. Barnett, F. L. "Chapter VI: The Reason Why." In: Wells, Ida B. *The Reason Why the Colored American Is Not in the World's Columbian Exposition*, 1893, pamphlet.
3. Palmer, Mrs. Potter. *Dedication and Opening Ceremonies of the World's Columbian Exposition*. Address Delivered by Mrs. Potter Palmer, President of the Board of Lady Managers, on the Occasion of the Opening of the Woman's Building, May 1, 1893. Published by Permission. Chicago: A.L. Stone, 1893.
4. Addams, Jane. *In the White City: Jane Addams Discusses the Social Settlement*. Chicago: Jane Addams Memorial Collection, n.d. Special Collections, University of Illinois at Chicago Library.
5. Eagle, Mary K.O., ed. *The Congress of Women, Held in the Woman's Building*. Chicago and Philadelphia: Monarch Book Company, 1893.
6. Feldman, Ann E. "Women Composers at the 1893 World's Columbian Exposition." *Notes, Quarterly Journal of the Music Library Association*, September 1990, Vol. 47, No. 1, 7–20.
7. The World's Congress Auxiliary of the World's Columbian Exposition. *The Woman's Branch of the Auxiliary*, 1892.
8. Elliott, Maud Howe, ed. *Illustrated Art and Handicraft in the Woman's Building*. Paris and New York: Goupil & Co., 1893.
9. Anthony, Susan B. *Moral Influence vs. Political Power*. Lecture at the Woman's Building. *Chicago Daily Tribune*, May 31, 1893, Roll 31:488 in The Papers of Elizabeth Cady Stanton and Susan B. Anthony, 1866–1873.
10. Cordato, Mary. *Representing the Expansion of Woman's Sphere: Women's Work and Culture at the World's Fairs of 1876, 1893, and 1904*. Ph.D. dissertation, New York University, New York, 1989.
11. Rydell, Robert W. *All the World's a Fair: Visions of Empire at American International Expositions 1876–1916*. Chicago: University of Chicago Press, 1984.
12. Sklar, Kathryn Kish. "Hull House in the 1890s – A Community of Women Reformers." *Signs*, Summer 1985, 658–677.
13. Weinman, Jeanne Madeleine. *Fair Women*. Chicago: Academy Chicago, 1981.
14. Croly, Jane Cunningham. *The History of the Woman's Club Movement in America*. H.G. Allen & Company, 1898.
15. Scott, Anne Firor. *Natural Allies: Women's Associations in American History*. Champaign, IL: University of Illinois Press, 1992.
16. Feldman, Ann. "Articles on Bertha Palmer and Ellen Henrotin." In *Women Building, Chicago, 1790–1990*. Rima Luymin Schultz and Adele Hast, eds. Bloomington: Indiana University Press, 2001.

3 Gender and Media

"Noteworthy Women": Use the Power of Media to Amplify Unheard Voices

It's challenging to break into mainstream media presenting previously marginalized voices. The key to building trust in that environment is to give your media partners and on-air guests what they need. Sometimes, it takes careful listening and a successful history of working together before they share their true wishes. Then, find a way to make your creative products respond to those needs.

In the 1990s, Artistic Circles developed *Noteworthy Women*, a national radio series about women in music. Produced for Women's History Month, the series was one of the first of its kind. These ten, one-hour programs featured female composers, performers, musicologists, and media personalities and were syndicated in the US by WFMT Radio Networks Public Radio and in Mexico by Radio UNAM.

The Power of Radio—The 1990s

I was delighted by the size of the radio audience we had reached with our production of the World's Fair women *Politics and Old Lace*. Winning the top award at the New York Broadcasting Festival put our program in front of additional listeners. This was a huge reach for our nonprofit Artistic Circles, far beyond academic or public programming or the usual nonprofit audiences.

I saw that radio power was the means to amplify the voices of unheard and overlooked women, and I intended to use it to full advantage. However, the reality of public radio was that each day local station programming was filled with nationally syndicated shows such as *All Things Considered*, locally produced news, famous hosts, and already entrenched successful shows. There was little room in the lineup for a new, unproven series, especially one about women and music.

DOI: 10.4324/9781003296423-4

Returning to WFMT

Fortunately, Marco Werman, host of WGBH's *The World*, gave me a tip, "They may need additional new programming for March. That's Women's History Month. Try to fill that niche with your radio shows." It was Golden advice. It answered the question of "when" to pitch our ideas.

The next question was "where?" I felt that Chicago's premiere classical music station WFMT was the answer. They had previously broadcast *Politics and Old Lace* and were pleased with the success of the show and the award it garnered. I contacted Associate Producer Lois Baum to brainstorm how I could convince WFMT to syndicate a radio series on women and music.

For our meeting, I came armed with materials from a course I was teaching at Northwestern University, called "Noteworthy Women." That course spanned a range of music from classical composers to blues, jazz, New World, and folk music. It also featured female musicologists who had devoted their careers to recovering women composers lost to history.

Lois was intrigued by my idea. We had a conversation that bounced back and forth between us like a ping-pong match, which became the model for future on-air interviews:

Ann: Shall we take the risk?
Lois: We'll take some risks with these programs, for sure. You have an inner energy and an inner spirit that won't be stopped, that won't take "No" for an answer. I love that.
Ann: I think it's remarkable that WFMT plays Schumann, Mendelssohn, and Mahler and only uses their last names. I want to talk about Clara Schumann, Fanny Mendelssohn, and Alma Mahler.
Lois: And you know, at this point, men aren't willing to accept any of that. Whether it is real history or not, whether it is documented or not.[1]

Lois was fully on board, but now it was time to approach the boss, Norm Pellegrini. He was the general manager and gatekeeper for Chicago's WFMT and a legend in the radio world.

The Pivotal Meeting—Fall 1994

Clutching my glossy bound notebook, I followed Lois into the inner sanctum of Norm's office. You didn't merely knock and enter; you had to be invited in. Norm sat regally behind his pristine desk. The only objects on its surface were a large program schedule, a row of sharpened pencils, and a black dial phone (this was pre-cellphone days).

Lois hovered around Norm, reminding him of the success of *Politics and Old Lace* and briefly telling him about my idea for a series of radio shows. Then, she deferred to me for the pitch. I began by listing the strong points for what I was calling *Noteworthy Women*: (1) much-needed programming for Women's History Month (March); (2) a terrific lineup of women composers and historians from classical, jazz, and blues worlds and from African-American, Mexican, and Chinese backgrounds; and (3) the new minority audiences that these minority composers and performers would attract. In the 1990s, such audiences made up only a tiny portion of public radio listeners, but they represented a huge growth potential for WFMT.[2]

Norm listened. As he nodded, I grew more eloquent until, finally, my passion overtook my good sense. "I'd like to start by featuring composer Wendy Carlos, who used to be named Walter Carlos, composer for *Tron* and *Clockwork Orange*. In the late 1970s, Walter had gender confirmation surgery to become Wendy."

At this point, Lois cleared her throat loudly, her eyes wide. I misunderstood and thought that I needed to put more passion into my pitch. I pressed on. "Wendy will be the ideal example to show gender bias in music, how music commissions nearly dried up after the gender confirmation." Norm raise one beautifully manicured hand, and I immediately stopped talking.

In his melodious voice, he offered, "WFMT will air four hour-long shows next March. We'll assume all the editing and recording costs. However, maybe you can put the Wendy Carlos show in the *middle* of the series?"

Exhaling in relief, I nodded as Lois grabbed my hand and quickly led me out the door. That was close. I'd let my personal passions cloud my good business judgment. If I wanted to succeed, I needed to learn to read the room and proceed cautiously.

The Plan for Noteworthy Women

Lois and I hammered out the nuts-and-bolts structure of the first four radio programs in her cramped office. Unlike Norm's spacious desk, hers was small and piled high with papers, reel-to-reel tapes, and cassettes. Floor-to-ceiling metal bookshelves overflowed with books and tapes. There was barely room for our two chairs.

Right away, my self-doubt started to kick in. "Should we hire an on-air host for the programs?" I asked. "No," Lois said. "It's your idea, your show, and you'll be the host. I'll help you." She taught me how to do interviews: "Research the subject, listen to their music, read everything you can get your hands on, and then condense it down to five questions. At the end, always ask the person what they'd like to add that you haven't discussed."

For the interviews, I decided that I would use the conversational, ping-pong style Lois and I had spontaneously developed.

We chose four women composer/musicologist teams for the initial series. We focused first on lyrical, classical music to appeal to WFMT's mainly White, middle-to-upper class traditional audiences.

The series would start with one of Norm's favorite composers—Shulamit Ran, the Chicago Symphony Orchestra's composer-in residence. Shulamit Ran was only the second woman to win a Pulitzer Prize in music. She was a passionate advocate for new music and an internationalist, having been born in Israel and traveled around the world.

Shulamit found a way to make modern music accessible and fascinating. While most composers often gave me a pat answer to the question of how they created a piece of music, Shulamit answered honestly and with humor: "I once conceived an entire symphony in 60 seconds. But then it took me six months to write it down."

For the show, I paired Shulamit with a controversial musicologist who was an aggressive feminist. They argued about equality for women in music. Shulamit felt that she hadn't personally experienced gender discrimination, while the musicologist argued that the system of music itself was unfairly biased in favor of the male gender.

The true magic of developing the series happened in the editing studio. We were able to create a point/counterpoint style between the two women, made famous initially by *60 Minutes* in the 1970s and *Crossfire* on CNN (1980s to 2014).

Editing takes a lot of time, but Lois never used a stopwatch or kicked me out of the studio. During my first editing session, I learned that radio production could be a highly spontaneous and creative venture. Try as I might, I could never stick to a script. I'd hear a certain inflection in an interview and know it belonged elsewhere. Lois didn't mind. As she told me: "[Legendary radio personality] Studs Terkel never used a script. He was never afraid to change his mind."[3]

The final show of the first season ventured away from the classical music to blues, featuring local Chicago African-American composers. We started with Florence Price, whose symphony was premiered by the Chicago Symphony Orchestra in 1933. But the real fun came when I interviewed blues artist Koko Taylor, one of my personal favorites with her smoky voice, rapid-fire laugh, and outrageous personality. I'd seen her perform numerous times at clubs in her signature sequined gowns and expected some of the same glitz at her interview. Instead, she came in casual polyester pants and top, with makeup that wasn't quite blended. Minutes before she arrived, I was dancing around the recording studio, listening to her irreverent song lyrics: "I'm a Woman – I make love to a Crocodile."[4]

We began with Koko's story of hardship and determination. She had traveled from the deep South to Chicago with only 25 cents in her pocket and a bag of Ritz crackers. I let her spin out the familiar tales I'd read again and again in her biography and in previous interviews. However, I wanted something that made her less of an icon and more of a person.

When the conversation became stale, I challenged her: "What did your husband say at the end of his life about your career?" Suddenly, the "canned" Koko was gone; instead, a determined woman looked back. "He sat up in bed, pointed at me and said, 'Keep touring and singing.'" Audiences loved her honesty.

Challenge of Building an Audience

Since this was one of the first radio series about women in music, we had our work cut out for us to market these programs. Each of the 350 NPR radio stations could choose whether to air the programs—there was little national programming. Marketing was going to be a time-consuming job. Carol Martinez, WFMT's in-house marketing director, was already over-taxed and didn't know the topic.

So, I came up with a plan of how to partner with WFMT to market our series. I already had a large national network of female composers, historians, and civic leaders. What if I matched the radio stations with my musical contacts in the same cities and pitched the idea of each station showcasing their home-grown talent? I offered to call each one of 350 stations in the Public Radio Network to sell the series. Carol let me try.

Right then, I learned a valuable lesson: Whenever possible, take some of the pressure off your media partners and shoulder it yourself—a powerful, trust-building strategy.

Carol sent out an email blast to the station managers and producers across the nation, announcing the *Noteworthy Women* series for Women's History Month. Then, she set me up in a cubby hole at WFMT with a list of the stations and contact information. I had a phone and a stack of Post-it notes and created a spreadsheet to keep track of all the calls.

Now, I needed a pitch—not too academic or preachy but explaining why the stations should air the series, which I believed was in their best interests. I came up with, "Imagine walking into a room filled floor to ceiling with beautifully wrapped gifts. Wouldn't you want to open them? That's the story of women in music – incredible beauty available for your audiences." The pitch worked.

I called every station two or three times until I got a "Yes" or "No" and built up a huge database of NPR contacts. On the phone and at radio conferences, I met fascinating Public Radio producers, hosts, and general managers from Alaska to Wyoming, from major universities to tiny colleges. I learned the difference between major markets in the big cities and small markets in little towns, college campuses, or community centers. All had their own stories to tell, and, usually, I was able to find common ground with them.

The result? In March 1995, 196 stations broadcast *Noteworthy Women*, reaching an Arbitron-estimated audience of 74,330,000 listeners. That was how radio power worked.

How to Build Diversity

With the success of the first series, WFMT gave me the green light for a second season. Funders and outside partners also became interested. It was time to get out of the studio and into the field to learn lessons directly from the participants in their own environments. I approached Chicago City Commissioner Lois Weisberg and asked for help to interview a successful group of female composers in Mexico. We needed to build on the diversity of nationalities, languages, and ethnicities for the radio series.

Interviewing in Mexico

Lois connected me with Chicago Artists International Program (CAIP), which funded my trip to the Festival Cervantino in Guanajuato, Mexico. It was the most important artistic and cultural event in Mexico and Latin America, attracting 200,000 visitors and 2,300 artists from 30 countries. Music by female composers Marcela Rodriguez and Gabriela Ortiz would be featured.

Why travel to Mexico, when I could interview the women by phone and already had recordings of their music? I wanted to see things from their perspective, to experience Mexican culture first-hand at the Festival. I believe that people are at their most authentic when you see them in their own environment.

I started in Mexico City, staying with internationally recognized composer Marcela Rodríguez. She introduced me to her composer friends— male and female. Marcela was a force to be dealt with. Her works were performed by leading orchestras and chamber groups around the world. At the Festival, I met more of her friends at the premiere of her symphony.

Again and again, I heard complaints about "Marianismo"—which meant putting women on a pedestal and not taking them seriously as professionals.[5] Although I had brushed-up on my high-school Spanish, I was grateful for the patience of the Mexicans as I conducted the interviews in both English and Spanish.

At the end, with the help of local Mexicans in Chicago, we produced the show in both languages for broadcast. The stations Radio Bilingue in California, Radio Esperanza in the Midwest, and Radio UNAM in Mexico broadcast the Spanish version to an estimated two million additional listeners. It was important to honor the culture of Mexican composers and reach to their special audiences.

The Musical Bridge: China and the US

By the second year of *Noteworthy Women*, I wanted to do a program on Chinese women composers and remembered the musician Chen Yi, who had been featured in my Northwestern University class. I assumed that funding the program would be easy but experienced surprising resistance from a major Chicago foundation. They explained, "We don't fund the Chinese community because they're so quiet. They don't make any heat for us, so we don't pay attention to them." I was upset by the denigration of a "quiet" community.

However, some Asian Americans had learned to overcome their reticence and fight for equal treatment. In the spring of 1995, Asian and minority students at Northwestern began a hunger strike and public protest to pressure the university to create an Asian-American Studies Program. At that time, I was Visiting Scholar in Gender Studies. That hunger strike and protest spread to other universities across the nation, and Northwestern ultimately agreed to establish the program, which took another four years to implement.[6]

I decided that 1995 was the perfect time to act. I discovered a way to use the beauty of music to stand in solidarity with the Asian-American students. I convinced the Dean of Northwestern's School of Music to host Chinese composers Chen Yi and Bun-Ching Lam as composers in residence. They would teach students to perform their music in a final concert.

The night of the concert, the performing hall was filled with students of color, especially Chinese. An Asian-American TV station filmed the concert for broadcast in the US and China, which made the evening even more glamorous. During that concert, I interviewed Chen and Bun-Ching about their experiences in China. This concert and interview became the radio program "The Musical Bridge: China & the U.S." as part of the *Noteworthy Women* radio series in 1996. It was the first time most of us had heard young women share their experiences of living through the Cultural Revolution of the 1960s. During that time, Chairman Mao Zedong had sent many artists, intellectuals, teachers, and professionals into rural areas to do hard labor. They were forbidden from practicing their arts and professions. Fortunately, Bun-Ching had been living in the Portuguese province of Macau and escaped that hardship.

Figure 3.1 Chinese violinist Chen Yi.
Source: Photograph by Chen Yi

Chen, however, lived in mainland China and was forced to do hard labor, hauling huge boulders by hand and hammering them into smaller pieces. She told us that she snuck her violin into her bag and played music for the other workers during lunch break. Chen Yi and Bun-Ching Lam awoke in me a deepening interest in China.

Gender and Jazz—1997

By the third season of *Noteworthy Women*, I was ready to tackle the composer who had originally sparked the idea for the entire series—Wendy Carlos. I was fascinated that Walter Carlos had achieved major success writing for movies and the *Switched-on Bach* albums, only to have commissions dry up after sexual confirmation surgery. I hoped that Wendy would talk about how women were excluded from the musical canon. This was years ahead of the Kardashian's Bruce Jenner becoming "Caitlin." At the time, there was little known about Transgender people.

I read everything I could about Wendy, including the 1979 *Playboy* article that revealed the sexual confirmation surgery.[7] The article went on to mention that in 1979, there were only 10,000 to 20,000 people in the US who identified as Transgender. The *Playboy* interviewer described in graphic detail the operation. Reading about it shook me. I had to come face to face with my own prejudices and concerns about sexuality and gender. I spent the next few months working to identify and rid myself of pre-conceived notions about what it meant to be a male or female. I met Wendy at their New York studio/home, since I wanted them to be comfortable. (Plural pronouns are often used by Transgender people to avoid gender labeling.)

When we first met, I noticed that Wendy had a pageboy haircut, wore a soft cashmere sweater and pleated skirt, and had a cat perched on her shoulder. Regardless of the comfortable setting, my own discomfort emerged during the interview. I stumbled over words and angered Wendy when I said that I wanted to focus on gender bias in music. Wendy snapped, "Do you want me to lift my skirt so you can see my gender?"

Mortified, I backtracked and told Wendy how much I enjoyed their compositions and asked if they suffered from a reduction in commissions after the operation. We discussed the growing number of Transgender individuals in the US, and the relative safety in "coming out."

Wendy gave an excellent interview and played the organ, synthesizer, and theremin for me in the apartment studio, which was crammed with equipment. At the end, Wendy asked me to sing/scream for the upcoming album *Clockwork Black*.[8] I was deeply honored and had a great time vocalizing on very high pitches with a great deal of drama.

For the radio program that included Wendy, we honored their desire to focus on music instead of gender. Wendy's presence alone on the program made an impressive statement.

Sisters of Choice in Jazz

Our third season of *Noteworthy Women* ended with the "Sisters in Jazz" concert, featuring pianists Marian McPartland, host of *Piano Jazz*, and local Chicago pianist Judy Roberts. Their decades-long friendship made the experience entertaining as I watched how much fun they had kidding around with each other as they worked.

By this time, I'd broken many of the rules of classical music radio programming. Why not do a program about sisters of choice—women friends sharing the common language of jazz? We persuaded the Chicago Cultural Center to host a live concert with this theme in their main hall under the Tiffany dome. The concert was open to the public, which meant that anyone could walk in off the street. As producer, Mike Orlove explained:

> The access was there – right in the center of downtown and it was free. But open to anyone meant just that. . . . You could also have homeless people attend the concert.[9]

The concert was a rousing success, with an overflow crowd. Those who couldn't get a seat perched on the stairs outside the hall.

"Sisters in Jazz" was the final show of Noteworthy Women. Over the three years of producing the radio series, I had learned about radio's beauty, flexibility, music, talk, context, conflict, and diversity. It was its own art form and had its unique power. Back in 1995, when African Americans, Mexicans, Chinese, and Transgender individuals weren't featured on mainstream radio – we used our platform to showcase their voices and personalities.

Today, diverse groups no longer need intermediaries to get out their message. Through podcasts and social media, anyone can make their own "radio" programs available to wide audiences. In 2020 alone, there were more than one million podcasts with over 29 million episodes.[10]

Noteworthy Women gave audiences the excitement of learning about diverse people—from rural US to Jerusalem, Beijing to Mexico City, Transgender, and Binary, avant-garde and classical, blues improv, and exacting notations. Our series became a conduit to connect composers, historians, radio engineers, and producers with millions of listeners in the US and Mexico. Audiences, producers, and radio hosts trusted us to bring them exciting new programming.

The "power of radio" experience had given me some important lessons:

- Learn how to fill a niche in programming.
- Involve academics, musicians, and media to reach audiences.
- Find supportive media partners and listen to them.
- Become actively involved in marketing your product—don't leave it to others.
- Build diversity into your programs; it makes them more interesting and broadens your audience.

Chapter 3 Case Study: Bias in Media and Society

Chitra Devare was struggling to find the best path for her career.

In summer 2021, the 20-year-old film major had just finished her junior year at a well-known East Coast university. Some months before, Chitra had won the Best International Short Documentary award from the Rising Talent Film competition based in New York City. Her entry, *See Us Now*, was a 30-minute documentary about LGBT+ teenagers in the suburbs of New Delhi, India's capital. As a lesbian herself, Chitra was elated about the recognition.

As part of the Rising Talent award, she had been given the opportunity to meet with established directors and producers of well-known documentaries and to hear their advice. "They were genuinely positive about my film," Chitra said, "and each encouraged me to expand it into a full-length documentary."

The idea resonated deeply with her vision and career plans, but Chitra was not sure how to pursue it, since creating a full-length film would require much larger financial support. She was reluctant to approach corporate foundations, especially those based in India, because she knew they had a record of exploiting workers. Also, while the film had been received well in Chitra's smaller, LGBT+-friendly circles, Chitra's extended family was uncomfortable with the subject matter, and a larger-scale project would probably cause more conflict.

Growing Up and Coming Out in Delhi

Chitra had grown up in the Delhi suburbs as the middle child between an older brother and an younger sister. Her father was a railway conductor and her mother was a homemaker. "My parents loved all of us deeply and did their best for us with limited resources," she said. That meant supporting Chitra's and her sister's schooling, despite ongoing cultural bias against girls' education. Chitra excelled in school, typically finishing ranked first or second in her large class.

The more challenging part of Chitra's life was on the personal front. "I knew from an early age that I was different." Accepting her homosexuality in a community that stigmatized it wasn't easy, but Chitra came out to her close friends in high school. She found support among them and also connected with a small group of local queer teenagers she found online.

As she gained a greater sense of identity, Chitra recognized that she would be happiest in a more accepting, progressive environment. She applied to universities in the US and won a full scholarship to an East Coast school with a world-renowned film department. When she broke the news to her parents, they were shocked and saddened. They said that they loved her but couldn't support her life choices.

New Life, New Project

Coming to the US was a major adjustment for Chitra, who had never been outside India. Although other Indian students were at the university, most were either born in the US or came from wealthy Indian families. "I felt different and was sad to find that there was still bias against me from some classmates for my gender, skin color, and sexual orientation," Chitra said.

Despite the bumpy start, Chitra soon found refuge in the LGBT+ group on campus. Their support, and the encouragement of her documentary film professor, motivated her to apply for a documentary-film sponsorship early in her junior year. She won the financial backing to make her first short film, *See Us Now*.

During winter break that year, Chitra returned to India for the three-week shoot in Delhi, working carefully around restrictions related to the COVID-19 pandemic. For material, she drew on the Delhi-based LGBT+ group she'd been part of, following three lesbian teenagers from different backgrounds, one of whom had been kicked her out of the house after her parents found her with her girlfriend. Shivani had been homeless during the documentary shoot. "That could have been me or any one of us," Chitra said. "It was important to me to show the lives of people like Shivani and all they go through."

How to Move Forward?

After being advised to expand *See Us Now* into a full-length documentary, Chitra considered her options. Although there were multiple possible funding sources, including those associated with large consumer goods and chemical businesses, Chitra knew that they had a history of exploiting workers and harming the environment. "With one hand, they do harm, and with the other, they offer help," Chitra said. "I'm not sure I can trust them." US-based foundations and nonprofits also offered support, but Chitra had little experience with these groups.

Finally, there was the matter of her family. "It has been hard for them," Chitra said.

> They love me but are reluctant to tell their friends about my sexual orientation and my projects. I worry that if my film becomes famous, it will cause a lot of stress for them, and I want to be mindful of that.

Questions to Consider

Imagine yourself in Chitra's shoes as you consider the following questions.

1. What different types of bias has Chitra experienced in her home country and the US? Are any of these surprising to you? Why or why not?
2. How can TV and film be used as a tool for advocacy for diversity on multiple levels? What challenges do producers of such content face?
3. What healthy perspective can Chitra maintain in advancing her film project?
4. Consider the possible sources of financial support Chitra might approach. What specific advice would you give her about how to choose

the right India-based sources, given her concerns? The right US-based sources? What might be the best strategies to gain their support?

5. How can you work with people you don't trust or who don't share your values related to diversity and acceptance? Can you find a common artistic ground? How?

6. How should Chitra approach her family and the distress her project might cause them? Is there a way for everyone to feel respected and valued?

7. Think about a project you might wish to gain support for. How can you apply the answers to the aforementioned questions to improve your chances of success?

Notes

1 Lois Baum, interview with Ann Feldman, December 3, 2018.
2 "Airing Questions of Access: Classical Music Radio Programming and Listening Trends," NEA Office of Research and Analysis, 2005, 3; "Black, Asian, Latino and White: Diversity at NPR," April 10, 2012, 6.
3 Baum, op.cit.
4 Koko Taylor. "I'm a Woman," in: *The Earthshaker* (Chicago: LP, Alligator Records, 1978).
5 Gil, Rosa Maria and Vasquez, Carmen Inoa. *The Maria Paradox: How Latinas Can Merge Old World Traditions with New World Self-Esteem*. Open Road Media, 2014.
6 Archival and manuscript collections, Northwestern University's Asian-American Studies Program, records 1993–2012, Identifier: 11/3/30/1.
7 Arthur Bell. "Wendy/Walter Carlos: A Candid Conversation," *Playboy Magazine*, 1979, 75–91.
8 Wend Carlos. *Tales of Heaven and Hell*, CD, East Side Digital, 2003.
9 Michael Orlove, interview with Ann Feldman, February 12, 2020. Orlove is the current Director of State, Regional, and Local Partnerships and of International Partnerships, National Endowment for the Arts.
10 "2020 Global Podcast Statistics, Demographics & Habits," May 23, 2020, published by PodcastHosting.org.

References

1. Block, Adrienne Fried. *Amy Beach, Passionate Victorian: The Life and Work of an American Composer*. Oxford: Oxford University Press, 2000.
2. Bowers, Jane and Judith Tick. *Women Making Music: The Western Art Tradition, 1150–1950*. Urbana, IL: University of Illinois Press, 1987.
3. Citron, Marcia J. *Gender and the Musical Canon*. Urbana, IL: University of Illinois Press, 2000.
4. Dahl, Linda. *Story Weather: The Music and Lives of a Century of Jazzwomen*. Pompton Plains, NJ: Limelight Editions, 2004.
5. De Barros, Paul. *Shall We Play That One Together? The Life and Art of Jazz Piano Legend Marian McPartland*. New York: St. Martin's Press, 2012.

6. McClary, Susan. *Feminine Endings: Music, Gender and Sexuality*. Minneapolis, MN: University of Minnesota Press, 2002.

7. Reich, Nancy. *Clara Schumann: The Artist and the Woman*. Ithaca, NY: Cornell University Press, 2001.

8. Solie, Ruth A. *Musicology and Difference: Gender and Sexuality in Music Scholarship*. Berkeley, CA: University of California Press, 1993.

9. Stein, Sammy. *Women in Jazz: The Women, The Legends & Their Fight*. Montreal: 8th House Publishing, 2019, 193.

10. Tick, Judith and Paul Beaudoin, eds. *Music in the USA: A Documentary Companion*. Oxford: Oxford University Press, 2008.

11. Sewell, Amanda. *Wendy Carlos: A Biography*. Oxford: Oxford University Press, 2020.

12. Walker-Hill, Helen. *From Spirituals to Symphonies: African-American Women Composers and Their Music*. Urbana, IL: University of Illinois Press, 2007.

4 Control

China & "Unbreakable Spirits": When You Fight for Others, You Fight for Yourself

> Sometimes, the truest control of artistic creativity is to listen to others and deliver their messages as honestly as possible. However, there are risks to relinquishing power. You may end up caught between competing forces in a culture. In creative work, particularly controversial work, your subjects are your responsibility and may need protecting at the expense of your own comfort or safety.

Artistic Circles' *Unbreakable Spirits* is a 12-part radio series about women and girls in China. Recorded in that country, it aired on Chicago's WBEZ. In the year 2000, it was syndicated nationally by Public Radio International (PRI) and also broadcast in China. Across the US, national educational programs coordinated with NPR's National Center for Outreach to present the series.

Unbreakable Spirits garnered a Gracie Allen Award from the Foundation for American Women in Radio and TV, and won a Special Conception for a Radio Program award from the Radio Shanghai Music Festival.

For the first time, US audiences were hearing from women musicians and composers in China.

China: A Beginning—1997

My life cracked open on the day I met a fortune teller in China. I heard him yell from a side alley, "Lady, lady, come here! Do you want to know your future?"

I forgot about the rotting goat hanging from a nearby stall, the colorful silks and scarves for sale, and the puppies and snakes in cages. I'm a sucker for anyone who can tell me something about myself, give me a magic clue to unlock my inner being. And besides, what could it hurt?

DOI: 10.4324/9781003296423-5

The small man with crooked teeth had me transfixed. I could have walked back in time looking through his eyes. A real-life Chinese fortune teller said: "Give me your hands, and I'll tell your future."

My hands rose to meet his as if they had a mind of their own. His rough, corded hands were those of a laborer not a mystic. He proclaimed, "Your life will change. It will be split in two this year. You may wed a new husband or change your job. But you will never be the same."

I paid him the few yuan and found my own hands were shaking.

Later, my companion, a hard-edged woman filmmaker, laughed, "You're a fool to believe anything he says." *Maybe she's right*, I thought. Or . . . maybe I should trust my instincts and the magic of the moment and be ready and willing to follow a new direction in my life.

The trip to China began in 1997 on a dare. When I turned in my report to Chicago Artists International Program (CAIP) for the Mexico trip, director Pat Johnson looked me in the eye and asked, "Ann, where would you like to go next?"

Without missing a beat, I replied, "What about China?" The previous project with Chinese musicians Chen and Bun-Ching had triggered my interest the country and its culture. But I hadn't known I wanted to go there until the words flew out of my mouth. Over time, I'd learned to trust these spontaneous statements—they often reflected my deepest desires.

For me, music was the key not only to delving into Chinese culture but to bringing it back to Americans. I wanted to record all kinds of Chinese music, including folksongs, an orchestra, protest songs, rock, and pop.

Even more than the music, I wanted to hear the stories behind the creation of that music directly from the women inside China. I would try to transform the recordings and stories into a series of radio shows—something that would be the first of its kind in the US.

Why now? Because since 1989, the main image that Americans had of contemporary China was of a country that turned its tanks on the people's pro-democracy movement in Tiananmen Square. Americans distrusted this militaristic and oppressive Chinese regime. My instincts told me that there was a different story to tell. I wanted to show another side, human and female, a side I'd glimpsed in the live concert, "The Musical Bridge: China and the U.S." at Northwestern University and broadcast on *Noteworthy Women*. Through that work, I'd witnessed the power of the Chinese women's resilience during the Cultural Revolution. The revolution was marked by ten years of chaos in China, where artists, intellectuals, and professionals were persecuted. Yet these women had managed to keep their music alive despite such oppression.

With that broadcast, I'd just put my toes into the water. Now, I wanted more, to dive into the real thing and experience China *in China*.

Figure 4.1 Chinese man standing in front of tanks at Tiananmen Square.
Source: Photograph by Jeff Widener © AP Photo

Pat really liked the idea. CAIP paid for flights to Beijing for myself and an audio engineer. We had a start—I was both terrified and excited.

Building Connections

But we needed more than airline tickets to succeed. Our project also required additional funding and partners, which set off the game of "Who knows who?" I began by determining which people and organizations had a history with China or with the local Chinese community in Chicago. That way, we could use their networking skills and relationship histories to launch our project into China and onto public radio.

The careful matching of projects, funders, participants, and partners to a particular nation or discipline became the anchor of all our projects. This strategy ensured that everyone who came to the table had a personal or professional interest that would keep them engaged. Interdependence built trust.

The next challenge was to find women in music inside China who would agree to be interviewed for the radio series. Here's how we accomplished this goal: my contact, Chinese composer Chen Yi, knew conductor Zheng Xiaoying, the first woman to ever conduct an orchestra and opera in China.

Chen also knew Zheng's daughter, Su, who was in the US as a professor at Wesleyan University in Connecticut.

I called Su Zheng to see if her celebrated mother in China would be open to an interview.

At the end of our call, Su quietly cautioned: "Your presence will stir up some excitement about women in music. It's virgin land. This is an issue people have never really looked at."[1]

It was a clear warning. But it seemed like something that I'd be able to handle. I had no idea how official government reaction would impact the entire project.

I dug deeper into my networks, contacting Chinese professors at Northwestern University. One professor suggested a reading list of the current books about culture and politics in China. As I began to read, two things disturbed me. First, there was the emphasis on "saving face" in Chinese culture.[2] What did that even mean? Chinese friends explained that men, especially men in power, needed to be in control and never be embarrassed. Second, the suicide rate among Chinese women was the highest in the world.[3] At the time, I couldn't understand how these all fit together, but later I came to realize the fragile nature of women's power, especially when it threatened men in control.

I also consulted friends who had been to China. One of them, Chicago-based mystery writer Sara Paretsky, had attended the 1995 World Conference on Women in Beijing. She warned me: "China is a third-world country, and it'll be stressful physically. But don't let it stop you; you'll be thrilled by the experience and will hear a lot of women's stories that will astound you. But," she added, "try to have someone there who is close to you emotionally."[4]

Following Sarah's advice, I contacted a young Chinese translator, Jane Hu, but she couldn't make her schedule work with the timing of the trip.

These warnings should have set off alarm bells in me, but at the time, I didn't understand their value. It was a clear case of failing to fully trust others' advice and, instead, relying on my own artistic and personal momentum.

To record the China interviews, I needed an audio engineer. Luckily, I convinced Jan Thompson, a documentary TV producer, to join me.[5] She'd produced *Hidden China*, about food and culture in China, and was also an expert audio engineer. Unfortunately, Jan did not speak Mandarin Chinese and was not familiar with women's issues there.

Next, more networking was needed to find the money to cover our costs of travel and purchase audio recording equipment. The wife of a friend in Chicago introduced me to her cousin, who worked for a billionaire and his company. They did business in China and had people based there. Her cousin and I clicked. As I began to tell her my idea, my passion for the project ignited a passion in her. She immediately took my materials to her boss and convinced him to back us and our project.

I will always be deeply grateful for her help in obtaining the funding that made the trip to China possible, but it was her sage wisdom and a piece of advice that literally saved my life in the end. Right before we left, she handed me a list of names and contact information of some of their top executives in Asia, "Just in case." I didn't think much about it at the time and tucked it into my packet of papers, but later it turned out to be a lifeline.

We cobbled the rest of the money together from a variety of sources, including a long-term backer, the Illinois Humanities Council. People continued to warn me about working in China, including the council's grants officer, Dennis Kolinski, an expat from Poland. He cautioned: "Ann, be careful. You will be followed throughout China. You won't know who they are, but they'll know your every move and conversation."[6] Even my mother warned me, "Ann, keep your mouth shut in China." "But Mom," I replied, "I have to talk. I'm doing radio interviews." It all seemed so cloak and dagger.

Being Afraid but Doing It Anyway

But as I went through layer after layer of bureaucratic permissions and forms for travel, for recording interviews, and for creating shows, the immensity of the challenge began to invade my every waking moment. When people talk about an adventuresome adult, they usually start with, "She was fearless as a child." That wasn't my story. As a kid, I was afraid of nearly everything—going outside, getting dirty, failing in school (even though I was a Straight-A student), and disappointing others. The only place I was fearless was sitting at a piano.

However, when I became an adult and I had a cause that I believed in, I could barrel ahead. I deeply believed that it was my job in 1997 to go to China, record women and girls, and create a radio series with their voices and stories. So, I set aside my personal limitations and followed the limitless possibilities in service to those women. It didn't mean I *was* fearless, merely that I could *act fearless*.

My core anxiety about China was that I would have so little control. The Chinese government would decide everything. They had the right to issue permits for travel, approve my itinerary, even check our audio equipment. Working from Chicago, with few contacts inside China, I had only three interviews set up in advance. That was not enough.

On Their Time, Not Mine

I'm a "get things done" kind of girl. I like to be in charge of a project. But this time, I would have to learn a different way to work. A wise professor advised me, "Chinese things take on a life of their own. I've learned enormous patience."

Could I learn to wait, trust the process? Patience is not in my nature. Yet now, I had no choice but to learn it again and again.

On October 14, 1997, I woke up early that morning, grabbed my suitcases and equipment, and finally boarded the plane to China with a wild and wonderful sense of adventure ahead.

First Stop—Beijing

The moment I set foot in China, it was clear I should have paid a lot more attention to the warnings of my American friends and colleagues.

On day one, as I entered my room at the hotel in Beijing, the bell boy kept pointing to the ceiling. What was he trying to say? Something about the light? The fan? The fire alarm?

None of these. He was trying to tell me the room was bugged. From then on, I had to assume that every room I stayed in was bugged.

But my excitement overrode my fears. I was in Beijing with a job to do. My engineer Jan Thompson arrived the next day, and we began the work, taping music and interviews. The first session was with a group of highly trained musicians who played traditional Chinese instruments set in a lovely, peaceful room with wooden slats and landscapes on the walls. The beauty of their music washed over me. When I heard the sounds of the artfully played, ancient clay flute, shaped like a bird, *this* was the China of my imagination.

The next morning, I sat down with China's first female orchestral conductor, Zheng Xiaoying. I guess I'd been expecting another wistful, delightful conversation about music. Zheng surprised me, confronting me with a taboo topic, "Do you know how I spent the Cultural Revolution?"

I'd been warned by many people to stay away from this difficult topic. The government would not approve our talking about it.

Madame Zheng had no such compunctions. She told me through words and gestures how important it was to keep the art of music and conducting alive. She kept on teaching even though it had to be in secret:

> I invited young orchestral conductors to my home to learn their trade. I would close the curtains. Then I held my finger to my lips, opened the score of a Beethoven Symphony, picked up my hidden baton, and would take them through the piece, bar by bar.

As I listened, chills ran up and down my spine. A raw, simple truth: This was more important and much bigger than I had expected. Zheng was a woman who followed her personal destiny and responsibilities as a conductor, defying the restrictions of the government and keeping her art alive by training her successors.

I was scared, yet deeply moved. Would she be the only woman to tell a story of resistance or would there be others? There were.

Madame Zheng sent me to meet another woman, a sweet, mild-looking 78-year-old composer, Qu Xi-Xian. She turned out to be far from a gentle old lady. When the Japanese invaded China in the 1930s, she had written, at age 19, the song "Ploughing in the Spring." It became the standard patriotic protest song against the Japanese.

I'd imagined that these artists would be meek and pliant, both politically and personally. They were not. I quickly learned to pay attention to what the women wanted to tell me, not what I expected them to say. But nothing prepared me in advance for the wild ride we encountered when we interviewed COBRA, China's first all-female rock band.

COBRA

It was October 31, Halloween night. Finding the rock band's location was like something out of a spy movie. We were told to show up at a certain place; we'd get there, then the phone would ring, telling us to go to somewhere else. This happened three or four times until *finally* we walked down a dark flight of stairs into our secret destination, a dingy, smoke-filled bar.

Figure 4.2 Five Chinese female musicians from the rock band COBRA.

Source: Photograph by David Iam © COBRA

And there they were—COBRA. Five young women smoking, sitting at the bar, and drinking hard liquor (a shock to my young female translators). The girls in the band had punk short hair and long red-dyed pigtails, hoops in their ears, and wore all black.

These women had experienced a lot of discrimination. The Chinese government censored their music. They weren't paid the same as the male rock musicians and had to be supported by their parents. One of their hit songs "1966," included references to "the Red Express" (i.e., Chinese communism) that "never reaches its destination." Also, "fanaticism and bliss—is it heaven or hell?"[7]

If I hadn't already gotten the message that COBRA were outliers, that fact was made crystal clear at the end of the evening when we tried to take a group photo with the band.

A young man ran in front of us, ruining the photo. This was no errant photo bomber. He was one of many "minders," or government spies, watching us who had now made himself known. One of the band members pushed him aside, and we got our photo. But how many others were there, silently, secretly following and watching us that I never knew about?

The level of risk escalated each time I interviewed an individual or group that had defied the Chinese government. Who was more at risk—the Westerners or the locals? A simple answer: the locals I interviewed. The sense of danger was coupled with a thrill I'd rarely experienced—defying the powerful. The Chinese women kept upping the ante at every turn.

As the trip continued, I wondered if I could tell these stunning stories on the radio in America without hurting these talented, brave, and honest women. It was a dilemma I would have to face when I returned home.

Second Stop—Shenyang, Chicago's "Sister City"

I was excited about going to Shenyang in Liaoning Province. The province was home to six minorities, and Shenyang was Chicago's official Sister City. I hoped to find authentic minorities and get the chance to record their ancient songs and music.

The reality was a shocker. The air in Shenyang was *pink*, I mean *pink* like the Pink Panther, or worse, that awful sticky pink insulation. And thick—you could hardly see in front of you. Pollution was a serious problem here.

Another shock—there were six-foot tall policemen in greatcoats and large hats everywhere. All the Chinese people I'd met so far were about my size. Obviously, this was a show of force, and I wondered why.

The next morning, we journeyed a few hours away from the Chinese urbanized pink air out to the countryside. Our translator explained that we were in the Manchu (Manchurian) territory, the first emperors of China.

This was the China I'd dreamed of. Along the way, I met a man who collected the ancient songs of the women shamans and healers. The next stop was in a beautiful farmland village where young people in colorful native costumes performed traditional songs and dances. We were enchanted, until their leader put out his hand, demanding money. (I didn't pay it.) It was all a show for tourists. I began to wonder if my instincts were wrong and that visiting these minority communities was yet another commercial add-on planned by the government.

Our final stop that day was at an empty temple. By now, we'd now seen so many temples that Jan and I hardly paid them any attention. Then, an unexpected idea popped into my head, "Who's the religious official here?" "A woman," our government guide replied. That's when my instincts went on high alert. Women weren't supposed to lead religious organizations in China, a country where religion was officially deemed the "opiate of the masses."

A stout-looking individual in blue pants and shirt came to greet us. "The Buddhist nun," whispered the translator. At that point, I knew that we'd found "radio gold." I trusted my instincts and told Jan to film the encounter.

But something was off. When I asked the nun to sing Buddhist prayers for us, the translator gave us her answer, "Yes, we are very happy here."

Clearly, the translator was trying to thwart this encounter. That's when I relied on the universal language of music. I sang out phrases of a Gregorian Chant. The nun laughed in recognition and motioned us to follow her into her private *kang*, or room.

She took off her cap, revealing the trademark shaved head of Buddhist religious leaders, and put on a crisp, saffron-colored robe over her pants. She added the *mala* necklace, which had the traditional 108 beads.

Then, she led us into the temple and showed us how to bow before the Buddha. Uncovering a bright red wooden turtle, she began to strike it like a drum. It made a *tock, tock* sound as the nun chanted, "*Namo, Ami, Tofu*" (Infinite light). It was a powerful moment. Gratefully, I gave a donation to the temple, and she and I took pictures together.

But when I offered the nun my business card, the translator stepped in to stop us. The nun stood her ground until the official deferred to her. It was obvious that our translator knew the nun well.[8]

From that point on, things got rocky with our Shenyang hosts, including the translator, two other officials, and the driver. I wanted to change the government schedule and stay with the nun for a few days. Her chanting and devotion deeply affected me. Not only was this a journalistic gem, but I related to the nun on a spiritual and musical level. What was the point of recording government-mandated song and dance troupes for radio, when I had a ground-breaking story about a female Buddhist nun who'd led her minority community for 50 years?

Figure 4.3 Buddhist nun chanting.
Source: Photograph by Jan Thompson

That was the moment when competing agendas turned dangerous. The government officials wanted me to keep to their schedule. Both Jan and I were determined to stay with the nun, who also wanted to continue our conversation. The translator was clearly torn but deferred to her government colleagues, who insisted that any plans had to be coordinated back at the Shenyang hotel, two and a half hours away from the temple.

What choice did we have? Even though we were paying for the driver and translator, we didn't speak the language, know the local customs, or understand how to navigate in this very foreign country. We finally yielded, but when we returned to the hotel, things turned even more sour.

The translator informed me that her government bosses were insisting that I keep to the prescribed schedule. If I didn't, Jan and I would be immediately expelled from Shenyang and sent back to the United States, at our own expense.

As long as we "kept with the program," everything was fine. We even tried to hire a private driver and translator, but everyone was either part of the system or afraid of the government.

And demanding to interview a female religious leader threatened the carefully crafted propaganda of the government. Inadvertently, we'd step far over the line into unsafe territory.

I was afraid both for Jan and myself and for the nun, who had the most to lose. Then, I remembered the list of Chinese executives our funder had given me. I looked for the executive in Hong Kong. Why Hong Kong? Because in 1997, China was a two-state government. Hong Kong was independent, and we could safely fly there and regroup.

I called the Hong Kong executive and told him our situation. He warned, "Don't further upset the officials in Shenyang, because they may be powerful enough to prevent you from ever coming back to China in the future. They can put black marks in your record."

He offered to host us in Hong Kong, if we could get there. His final piece of golden advice: "No confrontation. Stay calm. Talk calmly. Tell them Jan is being sent to friends in Hong Kong, say, for treatment for her leg. Be grateful. You have to leave because there is no money, and your engineer is sick."[9]

At that moment, it dawned on me how dangerous our situation was with no one to turn to in Shenyang. We would need to rely on our Chinese hosts to get us to the airport and hope that we, along with our audio equipment and tapes, would arrive safely in Hong Kong.

Following the exact protocol that the experienced Hong Kong executive advised, I booked our flights to the province.

That night Jan and I renamed the audio tapes with nondescript titles so they wouldn't arouse official suspicion. Jan hid the film of the nun in a small box she kept in her breast pocket. I hid some of the audio tapes in my bra. We called our families.

My daughter, Laura, thought it was a great adventure, "Mommy, how exciting! You're so famous that they invited you to Hong Kong." But my husband, Mark, asked if I was going willingly. "No," I said. "If I don't call you by the end of tomorrow from Hong Kong, here's the phone number of our corporate contact."

Mark understood. Nobody slept that night. I knew Jan would have to fake the suggested leg injury and hope it would be convincing. In the morning, she tied a scarf around her leg and practiced limping. She also crushed an aspirin and applied the powder to her face so that she'd look ill. We dragged our luggage down to the lobby for the 5 a.m. government van to the airport. Standing by was a policeman, just to make sure that we were on that van.

We got to the airport, hoping our luggage and equipment would be with us on the plane. As we were about to board, a tall American with a buzz haircut and Texas accent approached us. It turned out that he worked for the American Consulate in Shenyang. He hissed, "Do you know how much trouble you've caused?" Once we were all on the plane, he introduced us to his colleague, the director. They told us, "You should have called the Consulate. We could have helped."

We felt shame at causing them trouble, but we also felt a bit of pride at our risk-taking.

Third Stop—Unplanned Trip to Hong Kong

Hong Kong was quite a shock after being in remote villages (think of New York City on steroids). Everything you could imagine was for sale—food, sex, electronics, and drugs. This was the 1990s, and the first time I saw cell phones. Nearly everyone had one and couldn't stop talking, even on public transportation.

But our stay was hardly a rest. We had one last stop on our itinerary— Shanghai. Would we even be allowed to travel there? Had I blown it? For the next ten days, we anxiously waited for our new visas to travel to Shanghai for the famous Radio Shanghai Music Festival. We had entered our radio show, "The Musical Bridge: China and the U.S.," and were hoping for at least an honorable mention at the festival.

As the Hong Kong executive listened to our experiences in Shenyang, he offered this advice:

> I hope I'm not being presumptuous, but it will take ten years of visiting, making friends, and working in China for you to understand the big picture. To really know the Chinese takes a long time. They will open up more and more to you each time you visit. American journalists come here and produce sensationalist pieces. You inadvertently hit most of the hot buttons of China. They likely think you're with the FBI.[10]

I realized then that to the Chinese officials, we appeared to be looking only for controversial stories. To us Americans, the Chinese seemed overly controlling and paranoid. Any fragile trust we had built was shattered. As clueless Americans, we didn't know we'd pushed the hot buttons of religion, the Cultural Revolution, protest against the Japanese, rock music, and feminism.

Fortunately, our misadventure didn't cause a break in confidence or trust with the American corporation funding us or with the Hong Kong office. They helped protect our radio assets, covered our costs, and sent back home some of our equipment, along with the precious completed tapes we had recorded from Beijing and Shenyang. That level of support was a tremendous help as I navigated my new role as a daring journalist in search of important stories.

Happily, we were in luck. The Shenyang government had *not* put a black mark on our official record and our visas came through. We would be able to travel back to mainland China to Shanghai, where we could attend the Radio Shanghai Music Festival.

Fourth Stop—The Shanghai Radio Music Festival

The festival was an important event held at an impressive site. We stayed at a hotel next to the 80,000-seat sports arena and performance stadium where live concerts would celebrate the festival.

My friend from Chicago, Jane Hu, flew over to Shanghai to attend the festival, where she'd worked for many years. Once there, I met radio producers, general managers, on-air talent, and funders from 60 countries.

Between meetings, I conducted several interviews. The most important one hit a final hot-button issue I *should* have avoided but didn't—Tibet. In the 1950s, China had invaded and annexed Tibet, then tried to force the Tibetans to give up their faith and way of life. The Tibetans resisted fiercely, but a popular uprising in 1959 failed. Fortunately, the Dalai Lama and many other Tibetans escaped into India.

Through Jane Hu and her connections with Radio Shanghai, we were able to arrange an interview with singer Zhong Yong Zhuo Ma, with Jane translating. There were many reasons to interview Zhuo Ma, not only the beauty of her voice and power of her music but also the rarity of a successful Tibetan singer in Chinese culture. I found a couple of her CDs and was surprised by a reference to "longing for the white, snowy mountains" (of Tibet) and the way she incorporated Tibetan folk songs into her pop music.

Yet, oddly, one of things that impressed me about Zhuo Ma was her *perfectly straight, white teeth*. Obviously, she had had expert dental care and had probably worn braces—an expensive proposition. Those sparkling teeth made me suspect there was a complicated back story. Though likely trained in a Chinese music conservatory and lauded as a Tibetan musician, this young woman had managed to stay true to her culture.

The entire time I interviewed Zhuo about her music, a different set of internal questions kept distracting me:

> Was she a Tibetan Buddhist? How hard was it to be Tibetan and practice Buddhism while going to school with successful Han Chinese, who were the majority? Could she tell me anything about the nun I had met? Why was the Chinese government upset about me interviewing the nun?

I let Zhuo spin out the same story she'd likely told dozens of other interviewers. But my internal questions finally overrode whatever sense of self-protection I retained. I blurted out, "I need your advice about a meeting I had with a Buddhist nun in Shenyang. You see, the police threw me out of the city for interviewing her."

Suddenly, someone started banging loudly on her apartment door, and Zhuo Ma's eyes grew wide in fear. When she opened up, the vice president of Radio Shanghai stood in the doorway and announced, "The interview is over! Were you talking about Tibet?" Both Zhuo and I shook our heads, "No," but, by now, we should have known that her room was bugged.

Jane was clearly upset with this change of direction for the interview, and Zhuo seemed worried about herself. I wondered if Radio Shanghai would throw me out of the festival and send me back to Chicago, as the Shenyang officials had tried to do.

I waited one day, two days, and nothing happened. But that didn't mean that my actions hadn't caused a stir at official levels.

Jane explained why she thought the vice president of the festival might be upset.

> Ann, you are a foreigner, and they don't know your intention or what you want to do. You break their rules, ignore their pre-arranged schedule, and do something on your own that they perceive as improper. That's how the trust broke down. There are some taboo topics that the Chinese government doesn't want foreigners or journalists to touch or to report on, including religion, Tibet, and politics.[11]

Luckily, my *faux pas* didn't sour my relationship with Radio Shanghai. The city of Shanghai is and was a very different place from Shenyang. I continued doing interviews, attending sessions, and interacting with producers and general managers from the most prestigious radio stations around the world. Although I kept waiting for any repercussions from my interview with Zhuo, there were none.

As the festival's closing award ceremony approached, the excitement built. The festival would give out major awards to the top radio programs. The event, a major gala, would be televised, reaching millions of Chinese viewers.

On the day of the award ceremony, I was invited to join the other nominated producers in a private van to the festival and was advised to "dress up." I'd been on the road for six weeks in remote areas doing interviews and didn't really have appropriate fancy clothing. But I managed to find a long skirt and put on a clean sweater.

The festival was wonderful. We were ushered into the front row of a large auditorium like rock stars. On stage, tall, glamorous Chinese beauties paraded for the audience in elaborate hairdos and red sequined gowns that showed lots of leg. Video cameras were everywhere.

To the left and right of me, my foreign colleagues from the BBC, Radio Netherlands, and the Canadian Broadcasting Company were called up to the stage to accept their awards. Now, I was nervous. If I won an award, what would I do? I didn't speak Mandarin; I wouldn't even be able to thank the festival.

Then, I heard my name called. I had won one of the festival's top awards, which stunned me. A producer from the Netherlands whispered in my ear, "Get up there! And don't trip on the stairs up to the stage." The Radio Shanghai Music Festival awarded me an enormous, seven-pound bronze gong for "The Musical Bridge: China and the U.S."

The irony wasn't lost on me. Almost in the same week, I'd been kicked out of Shenyang and then won a top broadcasting award in Shanghai.

Fifth Stop—Chicago, Coming Home

When I returned to Chicago, I was both relieved to be safe at home, yet at the same time, disappointed that the grand adventure in China was over.

I was wrong—it was far from over. The experience of facing danger, of being forcibly removed from China with no visible safety net, triggered some crazy emotions, what I now know was PTSD. For months following the trip, there were times when I found myself shaking uncontrollably. I believed that my home and office phone lines were tapped. The fear of being monitored made me keep my emails noncommittal and bland.

And true to the fortune-teller's prediction, I had changed. There was a fire inside me to represent and stand for those Chinese women who had endured far worse than being asked to leave a country. Simply for being artists, these musicians and intellectuals had been sent to do hard labor for months, even years during the Cultural Revolution. And, in 1997, they were still being watched by the government. They all feared for their livelihoods, their families, and their own safety.

Despite this threat, they had talked to me. They had the strength and courage to tell me their stories and honestly share their struggles, along with their dreams and disappointments. The Chinese women relied on me to keep their stories and lives safe.

I would find a courage to match theirs. With that vow burning inside me, I reviewed the interviews and began to work on the radio series. These women were *Unbreakable Spirits*. I, too, would become one of them.

Right away, I was confronted with a major ethical issue. Jan, my audio engineer, urged me to write an exposé on our China trip for the *New York Times*, *The Atlantic*, or *The New Yorker*. I was concerned that such a public article could hurt the Chinese women I'd learned to care about.

I couldn't be reckless with other people's lives. Only our corporate funder knew the whole truth, as they had saved us and our precious tapes in Hong Kong. But they'd kept our secret.

I could write an article for the *Times* and have my 15 minutes of fame, but at what price? The Chinese consul had already sent me a warning message: "The Chinese government is angry with you."

Here, I was home, safely embraced by my city and able to use our national media to tell any story I chose. But it could endanger the brave and talented women I'd left behind. They didn't have the same safety net I did.

Needing advice, I called Professor Su Zheng at Wesleyan University. I asked her, "Would publicly telling her mother, Madame Zheng's, story on the radio cause difficulties for Su and Madame Zheng?" To my surprise, Su laughed and shared her own stories of all the illegal things she had done during the Cultural Revolution, such as secretly listening to pop music. But while the conductor Zheng Xiaoying was powerful, famous, and protected, the Buddhist nun was not. What price would she pay for my honesty?

I would not write a sensationalized article about being expelled from Shenyang. Instead, I would protect those women I'd grown to admire and love in my six weeks in China. These women—with their honesty, secrets, steadfastness, and quiet passion—had given me gifts and taught me the biggest lesson of my life: Others cannot break you if you have the spirit to fight back.

My focus would be on bringing the women's art and music to the forefront. I'd highlight the 50 years of the nun's devotion to her minority community, the creativity of the conductor who learned to teach in silence, the hard-edged tenacity of the rock singers who spoke truth to power.

I became unbreakable and *unstoppable*. I set to work with a vengeance, approaching funders from large to small, confident I would get the money.

But nothing clicked. It was obvious that I needed a new strategy.

Show Don't Tell: The Demo

The new strategy was to create an audio demo for the radio stations and funders I wanted to reach. My preference was to begin the demo with the story of the nun and Buddhism in China, but I understood that a general audience might not resonate with that as the lead. It was probably best to use something more mainstream, upbeat, sexy, and tantalizing, so we opened with our interview with China's number one pop singer, Zhu Hua.

Zhu wasn't merely a bubble-headed beauty. She had trained as a classical singer with an uncanny sense of how to get around the Chinese censors. For her number one hit song "Fantasies of the Mind," she made the female character Arabic, not Chinese. That way, the lyrics could reveal a deep sensuality without threatening Chinese moral standards.

Finally, in September 1999, after ten months of pitching the project, I got a "yes" from the radio station, WBEZ-FM in Chicago. They agreed to partner with us for a 12-part radio series called *Unbreakable Spirits*, as part of their public radio station's new morning show, *8:48*.

WBEZ had never featured Chinese stories and Chinese women. For that matter, neither had any other mainstream stations. On top of that, *8:48*, a brand new, 90-minute morning program, was just finding its way. The producers wanted content that combined local, national, and international angles, and *Unbreakable Spirits* fit that need.

Steve Edwards, the host of *8:48*,[12] recalls being surprised at the excited audience response to the series.

> Clearly the stories were the most important thing. For our audiences, it was illuminating to hear from women in China and to learn about their varied life experiences and artistic practices. You were taking audiences inside the homes, communities, places, and disciplines on a journey they had never experienced before. It also signaled to Chicago's Chinese-American communities that we were a station that was interested in their lives and experiences.[13]

By sharing authentic stories recorded in China and broadcasting them over WBEZ, we proved to minority audiences that we cared about and valued their communities and heritage. In turn, they trusted us with their time and listenership.

In 2000, *Unbreakable Spirits* was syndicated by Public Radio International (PRI) and was now heard by millions of people on hundreds of local public radio stations across the US. I also learned that the series was broadcast in China. In addition, we partnered with National Center for Outreach to create educational programs using the radio series.

What did all this mean for the Chinese women in our series? It gave them an opportunity to have their stories, music, and lives heard and validated through mainstream media.

What did it mean for Chinese audiences? Their experiences and traditions were honored. At that time, less than four percent of Asians listened to public radio.[14] Jane Hu told me:

> You used music as the transcendent bridge over politics, culture, or language. It is a very powerful thing. And what impressed me, even as a Chinese-American living in the U.S. for quite a few years, was that we were reintroduced by you to what was happening in China through your perspective and getting to know those Chinese rock stars, pop stars, concert music composers, and Tibetan singer and monks.[15]

Bringing unknown voices to a previously invisible Chinese public was my overriding motivation. Perhaps, it resonated so deeply because my own voice was often suppressed, and I had often questioned its worth. While I might not have the courage to value my own voice, I was tenacious in presenting the voices of others, especially women.

Fight for Others, and You Fight for Yourself

Each time I fought for the Chinese women to be heard, I became stronger. Nothing happens in isolation. As I built up my strength on their behalf, I also started to battle for my own right to express myself.

Why do organizations like CAIP support artists like me to go overseas to discover and bring back these stories from foreign countries? Grants officer Sofia Zutautus explained,

> You received the award because of your professional caliber, Ann. Here in America, we are so isolated. We are protected. You were affected by the country. There was a dynamic there you were not expecting. I'm sorry for your bad experience [being expelled from the country], but happy it happened, because that's what this program is all about.[16]

It is always transformative to step into someone else's shoes. Through that visceral, gut-wrenching experience in China, I got a taste of what it was like for these remarkable women to live under government surveillance and restrictions. That's why I view what happened in China as a gift. People have asked me, "Were you scared?" Yes. "Would you do it again?" Yes. "If you could, would you change anything?" *Never!*"

Chapter 4 Case Study: Who's in Control?

Kwan Gaon needed to take control of her music and her life.

The 19-year-old South Korean native had lived in the US since age 14 and was now majoring in Radio, TV, and Film at the University of Texas in Houston. A long-time musician, Kwan, played in an all-Asian female rock band that had become popular on campus and in the surrounding region, performing multiple paid gigs each month.

But Kwan and her bandmates were facing increased prejudice and harassment, based on anti-Asian hate, in the venues they played. One member was ready to quit, but Kwan wanted to continue playing, given her passion for the music.

Unsure of how best to take control, she thought back on the road that had led to her present situation.

Gaining Early Strength

Kwan was born in South Korea to parents who purposely named her for the combination of *strength* (Kwan) and *calmness* (Gaon) they saw in their baby daughter. Despite her diminutive size and soft voice, Kwan exuded fierce determination.

Things changed when Kwan turned 14. Her parents decided to send her to school in the US "They wanted a better education for me," she said. "But I had to leave everything I knew for a new country, language, and culture." Enrolled in an elite boarding school on the East Coast, she quickly realized what it meant to be an outsider without nearby family support. With a serious language barrier, no social connections, and trained in a different educational system, she did poorly in school at first and made few friends.

Her one great passion was playing electric guitar, which she did often in her room and her dorm's common areas. Her dormmates took notice; and at the end of her freshman year, Kwan was invited to join a four-member girls' band, which included two sisters who had friends in Kwan's dorm. Kwan was the youngest member and loved playing with them but faced challenges getting to and from rehearsals and shows:

> We played in the city, far from my school. I took a bus and train to get to each practice or show. The shows ended really late, so I had to either ask one of their parents to drive me or take a train home. And when I got back to school, it would be very late at night.

The father of the sisters used his network to try to get the band gigs at local bars and clubs, but it wasn't easy as the girls were underage. "I understood their hesitation, but at the time it felt like we had no voice, and nobody wanted to listen to us."

Kwan's participation in the band continued until soon after she turned 16, when the other members gently told her that they had found a new guitarist who was 18. "They were now old enough to play in bars without any issue. But it was heartbreaking because of how much I enjoyed playing in the band and how hard I worked for it. I felt disposable after that."

Taking Control

After graduating from high school, Kwan won a scholarship to the University of Texas Houston. She gravitated toward other immigrants and people of color as she pursued her education and worked on projects in music and film.

Soon Kwan discovered an Asian female band on campus and auditioned, winning a spot as lead guitarist. "It was nice being with others like me who loved music but had parents who wanted us to follow conventional paths like law or medicine," Kwan said. "We bonded around that shared experience."

The band developed a solid reputation on campus and in the general region, winning opportunities to perform gigs at local venues. Still, the band faced increasing challenges playing for a wider range of audiences. While most people were respectful, some who attended the shows were overtly prejudiced, booing the band and yelling racial slurs, especially during COVID-19. On several instances, inebriated bar patrons followed the band members outside after the show and security had to intervene. "It was scary," Kwan said. "We were just there to play and didn't expect to encounter that kind of thing. We weren't sure what to do."

One of Kwan's bandmates felt like quitting because of the harassment they faced. But the other two were committed to the band. "They said we have to be strong," Kwan said. "I agreed but wasn't sure exactly how."

Questions to Consider

Put yourself in Kwan's place as you consider the following questions.

1. What are the main pressures and prejudices Kwan faces in the US? In Korea?
2. How can Kwan try to take control in the situation she finds herself in? How might she convince her bandmates to follow her lead, especially the one who has threated to quit?
3. Which supportive friends can the band members ask to help them get home after late shows, for example?
4. Now, think about an area of your life where you feel like an outsider and answer these questions:

   • Who has control in that situation and who doesn't? Whom do you trust?
   • What approaches can you use to take back control? What have you already tried? What worked?
   • What kind of leader are you? Do you prefer being in control of others or do you work more collaboratively? What are the pros and cons of each style?

Notes

1 Su Zheng, Music Department, Wesleyan University. Interview with Ann Feldman, personal Day-timers Journal, August 30, 1997.
2 Perry Link. *Evening Chats in Beijing* (New York: W.W. Norton & Company, 1992), 3–50, Introduction.

3 Jianying Zha. *China Pop: How Soap Opera, Tabloids and Bestsellers Are Transforming a Culture* (New York: New Press, 1996), 157.
4 Ann Feldman, from personal Day-timers Journal, August 21, 1997.
5 Jan Thompson, former professor Southern Illinois University film department. Producer of film *Hidden China*, 1992, part of the *Hidden Journey* series.
6 Ann Feldman, personal journal entry, "Making Space for Myself and Growing a New Skin," July 8, 1997.
7 Yuwu Song. *Biographical Dictionary of the People's Republic of China* (Jefferson, NC: McFarland Press, 2014), 368.
8 Ann Feldman, personal China Diary, June 11, 1997.
9 Ibid.
10 Ibid.
11 Jane Hu, interview with Ann Feldman, May 7, 2020.
12 Steve Edwards, Vice President and Chief Content Officer of Chicago's premier NPR radio station, WBEZ.
13 Steve Edwards, interview with Ann Feldman, December 13, 2018.
14 Edward Schumacher-Matos. "Black, Latino, Asian and White: Diversity at NPR," NPR Report, April 10, 2012.
15 Hu, op.cit.
16 Sofia Zutautus, interview with Ann Feldman, May 21, 2020.

References

1. Link, Perry. *Evening Chats in Beijing*. New York: W.W. Norton & Company, 1992.
2. Zha, Jianying. *China Pop; How Soap Opera, Tabloids and Bestsellers Are Transforming a Culture*. New York: New Press, 1996.
3. Song, Yuwu. *Biographical Dictionary of the People's Republic of China*. Jefferson, NC: McFarland Press, 2014.
4. Schumacher-Matos, Edward. *Black, Latino, Asian and White: Diversity at NPR*. NPR Report, April 10, 2012. www.npr.org/sections/publiceditor/2012/04/1 0/150367888/black-latino-asian-and-white-diversity-at-npr.
5. De Kloet, Jeroen. "Living in Confusion, Remembering Clearly – Chinese Rock." In: Mitsui, T., ed., *Popular Music: Intercultural Interpretations*. Kanazawa: Kanazawa University & Hoyu Printing, 1998, 38–51; also published in: *Crawdaddy*, Encinitas, No. 18, 1–4, 1997; Heberer (Hg.), Ostasian-Pazifik – Yaogun Yinyue: Jugend-, Subkultur und Rockmusik in China, Trierer Studien zu Politik, Wirtschaft, Gesellschaft, Kultur, LIT Verlag, Hamburg, 1994, 170–180; "Nichts als Vergnügen? Jugendliche Subkultur und Rock in China." Thomas 6; "To Seek Beautiful Dreams – Rock in China." In: *Oideion On-Line*. Leiden: IIAS, Leiden University, 1998.
6. Zheng, Su. "Music Making in Cultural Displacement: The Chinese-American Odyssey." *Diaspora: A Journal of Transnational Studies*, Winter 1994, Vol. 3, No. 3, 273–288. DOI:10.3138/diaspora.3.3.273.

5   Identity

The "Eternal Feminine": Defy Traditions to Create Social Change

> Back in 2000, classical music venues rarely played music by women composers. The general belief was that women's music was mediocre. We upended that belief with a concert devoted to 300 years of music by women composers. We included pre- and post-concert discussions about the eternal feminine, asking who defines women— men or women? We built trust with women composers, performers, historians, directors of nonprofit foundations, and audiences. In the end, our Grammy-nominated CD showcased the excellence and power of music by women.

In August 2000, "The Eternal Feminine" was the first concert at Martin Theatre in Chicago's Ravinia Park devoted solely to music by women composers. Ravinia was the summer home of the Chicago Symphony Orchestra. At that concert, Artistic Circles also held pre-concert roundtable discussions with the Illinois Humanities Council, scholars and audience members, and a post-concert Q & A with women artists and historians.

The concert resulted in *The Eternal Feminine*, a Grammy-award winning CD (KOCH International); a newly commissioned song cycle by composer Libby Larsen (*Love after 1950* published by Oxford University Press); and a national public radio program on WFMT Radio Networks.

Woman: Muse or Creator?

I was sitting in a darkened concert hall, luxuriating in the glorious sounds of baritone Mattias Goerne with his rich low tones and nearly feminine high notes. As he sang one of the great song cycles, *Frauenliebe und Leben*, by the great composer Robert Schumann, all seemed right in the world. But a nagging question disturbed my musical reverie.

DOI: 10.4324/9781003296423-6

Why was a *man* singing a song cycle written for a *female* voice? And why were the songs, which focused on women's love and life, written by a man (Robert Schumann), instead of his talented wife Clara? I realized then that the only music we heard in concert halls were compositions written by men. While Artistic Circles had helped expand radio programming to include women and minorities, concert halls remained stubbornly mired in the 19th century exclusion of women from the musical canon.

We had produced and created seven years of programs about women and the arts. Now, I wondered, *Where were the women composers in live performances? Were they merely the Muses for men or were they viable artistic Creators in their own right?* For the World's Fair women's project, we had highlighted both the government's acknowledgment of women and the women's revolution for social change. For the China project, we had reported on women's sacrifice of their public arts and private music-making during the Cultural Revolution. In Mexico, men insisted on putting women on pedestals, and women stepped right off them. For our *Noteworthy Women* series, we had told the story of Wendy Carlos, who had undergone sexual confirmation surgery and paid the price in lost commissions.

The battle to define women was one for the centuries, from Goethe's *Faust* to Picasso's paintings. As Robert Schumann's music poured over me, I began to daydream: What would happen if we created a concert of women's music and texts, sung by a woman? In my 39 years of attending thousands of concerts at halls, large and small, the only music I'd heard written by women was performed at eclectic "women's concerts" or as the rare "showcase" piece played by a symphony.

As I pondered this reality, an exciting idea began to take shape. Maybe I *could* do something about giving women their rightful place in the concert hall.

For this idea to succeed, we would need an attractive location, a celebrity singer, and strong partners. I started by approaching super-star Susanne Mentzer, the mezzo-soprano featured on Artistic Circles' *Women at an Exposition* CD. With an international career as an opera singer, a discography of dozens of CDs, and another career as a teacher and an arts advocate, Suzanne was perfect. She was smart, funny, and a maverick. When I asked her to headline a concert of 300 years of music by women, Susanne immediately agreed. She suggested Ravinia Park's intimate Martin Theatre as a venue and arranged a meeting with Ravinia's director, Zarin Mehta.

Before the meeting with Zarin, I had Susanne define the concert. As a mother, she chose themes of love and loss:

> I want to have control over what I choose to sing, I also want to feel that the poetry is an extension of myself – Susanne – as opposed to when

you're in an opera singing the character's words.[1] I need to be able to communicate the poetry as if I wrote it.[2]

Susanne and I met with Zarin Mehta at his Ravinia Park office. Thrilled to see Susanne, he obviously had a great admiration for her artistry. He agreed to a women's music concert, a first for Ravinia, and gave us a tour of the hall, an art deco jewel with gorgeous acoustics and an 850-seat capacity. Zarin warned me, "You'll never get an audience," to which I smiled and replied, "You'll see. The concert will be sold out."

When Susanne suggested the theme of women's life, loss, and motherhood, Zarin objected, "Motherhood is too obvious. Does it need a historical relationship other than topical? My concern, thematically, is that it may not be the greatest music. I never have a theme. That is only for critics."[3]

Undeterred, Susanne began her search for music that would suit her interests and voice.

Meanwhile, I met with long-time partners at the Illinois Humanities Council, who were committed to using the humanities and arts to spark challenging conversations among diverse people. They suggested, "What about a pre-concert roundtable discussion, outdoors in Ravinia's beautiful park?" Together, we chose the topic "The Eternal Feminine," a nod to Goethe's *Faust*: "The Eternal Feminine uplifts us all."

How did that proposed concert model apply to present-day, male-centered hierarchies in music, the arts, education, economics, history, science, and politics? We sent that challenge to women scholars nationwide. Their answers came flooding back. Experts from around the country wanted to join us.

By the end of 1999, we had a location, a celebrity singer, and strong educational partners. But we still needed one more element to make the evening memorable. To spark interest from the press and truly showcase Susanne's immense talent, we chose to commission a new song cycle written specifically for Susanne. After securing financial support, I sent Susanne the names of several women composers and recordings of their music.

Susanne chose Minnesota composer Libby Larsen, a master in writing for the female voice. Like a blind date, I took Libby to Susanne's home to discuss how they would work together to create the song cycle. I was thrilled when they immediately clicked, sharing a risqué sense of humor and a love of words, sounds, and varied styles. They talked in depth about poetry. Susanne wanted something contemporary, rejecting Libby's ideas of a Mae West melodrama, or Martha Stewart, or even Harriet Beecher Stowe. I could see that the two of them trusted the process of collaboration, and, most importantly, they trusted each other's skills to co-create the best possible musical composition.

Libby went on a massive poetry hunt, seeking poems that explored "issues of strength and centeredness and femaleness . . . in post-1950s American English." Libby believed

> that boldness translated into major ATTITUDE in the concert hall. Frau love 'em and leave 'em. It does come out of those emotions, but we don't wear corsets anymore. We were looking hard for [poetry that spoke to] the "Un-corseting of Women."[4]

This was a reference to the 19th-century fashion of women wearing corsets, an undergarment reinforced with whalebone slats and designed to give women tiny waists when they were pulled so tight women could hardly breathe.

Through trial and error, Libby and Susanne learned to match text, music, and emotion, creating the song cycle *Love after 1950*.

August 2000—"The Eternal Feminine" Events

So many questions about this project were firing off in my head. Could we actually sell out the concert? Would the audience like the new music? What about the critics' response to the entire evening and the quality of the recordings? And would the weather hold? There was possible rain in the forecast for the outdoor discussions preceding the concert. I was a wreck. Fortunately, my colleagues were not only calm and sane but also fully supportive.

At 5 p.m., on a clear, warm August evening, we started off "The Eternal Feminine" concert with outdoor roundtable conversations. Each table had eight participants and a leader with a set of questions. I was nervous and kept circulating among the tables, overhearing some spirited conversations: One scholar asked:

> Is the Eternal Feminine even relevant today? In a poem, it's wonderful. And when you take it out of context, sometimes it's galvanizing and other times within six months, it becomes like Scotch tape, and everybody thinks they know what it is.[5]

A male participant complained we'd translated the German incorrectly and that the phrase really was, "*Eternal-LY Feminine*." One of the music historians added: "For me, the Eternal Feminine is about the enduring contributions and creativity of women. For heaven's sake, you never look at a concert program with works written by men and say, 'Oh boy, I am really tired of this!'"[6]

The consensus of all the groups was clear: Women should define their own identities and not be defined by others.

Connecting with the Audience

About an hour later, we brought the roundtable discussions to an end and entered the hall for the concert. As I had boldly predicted, the hall was packed to capacity, and there was a buzz of excitement among the audience. Seated up front were the music critics from Chicago's two largest daily newspapers—the *Chicago Tribune* and the *Sun-Times*. My stomach fluttered with excitement and worry. The concert was out of my control now and in the capable hands of Susanne and her accompanist, Craig Rutenberg.

I needn't have worried. From the beginning, Susanne's lush mezzo voice, artful musicianship, and crystal-clear diction enthralled the audience. She began with traditional love songs in the styles of the great lieder composers, Schumann, and Mahler. But these songs were by *Clara* Schumann and *Alma* Mahler. Then, Susanne switched to more far-ranging pieces, choosing an English song about being lured to the sea by a sea creature. This time there was a twist to the story—instead of a mermaid luring a sailor, this time a seal man lured a woman into the sea where she drowned.

After the concert, Susanne explained to the audience why the poem was so meaningful for her: "I've been lured by men—guys who talked me into stuff and dragged me into the sea with them. I could identify with it."[7] She also sang beautiful lullabies, some composed by a student of Brahms, Lisbeth Alexander-Katz (the great-grandmother of Susanne's friend). These compositions focused on women's empowerment through love, loss, and motherhood.

The rest of the program blew conventional recital repertoire out of the water. Libby Larsen's song cycle *Love after 1950* was unlike anything any of us had heard in the classical concert hall. Sex was now front and center, with delicious lyrics by female poets and new renditions of the blues, torch songs, honky-tonk, and tango, along with Isabella Duncan's modern dance.

The blues song "Boy's Lips," from a poem by Rita Dove, sizzled with Susanne's rich mezzo voice and sensual diction—"A boy's lips are soft as baby's skin." Libby talked about the unique quality of voice that she used to showcase in that piece:

> It's the octave skip in "Boy's Lips." It has that quality like one of those mirrors where you see yourself repeated infinitely. "Ah, Ah" – THAT is mezzo![8]

But what brought the audience to its feet was good old American honky-tonk rock. Most of us identified that style with "Honky-Tonk Woman" by the Rolling Stones, with men sexually fixated on a woman.

"Beauty Hurts," text by Kathryn Daniels, brings power back to women. As pianist Craig Rutenberg pounded out the honky-tonk piano, Susanne hammed it up, complaining of "yanking a hank of my lanky hair around black wire-mesh rollers whose inside bristles prick my scalp like so many pins."[9]

Libby described what she hoped to achieve in choosing the poems and songs, some of which she had written. For example:

[My song] "Big Sister Says" pushes women off the pedestal. The OBJECTIFICATION of musical forms in our culture is, in some ways, INSIDIOUS. I tried to conjure up musical objects and paired them with a poetic object to study that particular view of sexuality. [10]

The audience loved the results and laughed out loud at some of the lyrics, an unusual sound in a formal concert hall!

At the end of the concert, no one wanted to leave. We'd built a community, first through conversation and then through women's music. But there was one more event: A follow-up post-concert discussion with Susanne, Craig, Libby, and several of the historians. This was also a first for Ravinia, an intimate way for audience members to personally ask their questions and hear the answers. Some questions couldn't be answered easily: "Why are there fewer untenured female professors at the universities? Why don't we hear more music by women in the concert halls?"

But we *did* hear about the personal connections among the historians who'd rediscovered female composers from other eras. One member of the audience asked, "Why do you bother with all these unknown women composers?" Dr. Judith Tick of Northeastern University answered:

We were struggling with this oppressive attitude and standards they [male historians] used from the past to block our ears. Beethoven was thrust into our ears, not to open them but to block them. And we were trying to open them because we couldn't hear the way they wanted us to hear and have a role in musical life.[11]

After the concert, we were one step closer to taking back not only *how* we hear music in the concert hall but *what* music we hear. We could change the game by choosing themes that meant something in our lives, like love and loss, but expressing them from *a woman's point of view*.

Rave Reviews for the Concert

John von Rhein from the *Chicago Tribune* recognized "The Eternal Feminine" as an important work and named our concert as one of the ten best of the year: "Throughout the ages, most depictions of the Eternal Feminine have been by male composers, artists and writers: think of Goethe,

Schumann, D.H. Lawrence, Mahler, Berg, Picasso. Much of that, fortunately, has changed with the coming of modern feminist studies and the
consequent tumbling of old sexist barriers."[12]

But the critic who really understood the events was Wynne Delacoma of
the *Sun-Times*:

> The evening offered the pleasure of discovery. The recital's greatest
> pleasure, however, was the thought that went into its musical choices
> and formats.[13]

"The Enternal Feminine's" Legacy

The concert also led to the production of a Grammy-nominated CD, *The Eternal Feminine*; the published song cycle *Love after 1950*; and an hour-long,
nationally syndicated radio program that combined the conversations, music,
and Q & A from the concert. Since that time, *Love after 1950* has become
standard repertoire for singers in college. Libby and Susanne still give master
classes together at the Songfest festival at Texas A & M University.

Figure 5.1 CD cover of *The Eternal Feminine*.

Source: Entertainment One

Libby and Suzanne's collaboration has lasted more than 20 years and produced another song cycle, *Sifting through the Ruins*. Their shared respect, humor, curiosity, and belief in students led them to mentor college students and expand the repertoire that singers choose to perform in concert halls and other venues.

We had succeeded despite others' doubts. *The Eternal Feminine* took a stand for the power of women to define their own identities. For women to "un-corset" themselves, they not only needed to uplift others but also to free themselves.

The whole experience had taught us some unforgettable lessons that could benefit others who wanted to create ground-breaking programs:

- Put together a winning proposal so that the power brokers can't say "no" to your ideas.
- Trust your partners and your own gut on how to proceed.
- Combine the talents of musicians, academics, and media to provide innovative experiences for audiences.

Chapter 5 Case Study: Dealing With Identity Bias

Angel Rodriguez faced a major identity challenge.

The 24 year old was a Cuban-American Ph.D. student in Education at the University of Miami and a student teacher at a local high school.

Early Identity Challenges

Angel had struggled with gender and sexual identity from an early age, eventually identifying as gender non-Binary (preferred pronouns: they/their). "As a kid, I realized my identity fluctuates and doesn't conform to traditional gender roles. I think of myself as non-Binary, queer, and one hundred percent Angel."

Angel was born to Cuban immigrants and grew up in the suburbs of Miami. "Our extended family was very loving, and we spent a lot of time together." But Angel, assigned a male gender at birth, recognized from an early age that this descriptor was not accurate.

> My family wanted all the boys to be strong, dominant men who never expressed their feelings, like my dad and uncles. I was soft-spoken, obviously effeminate, and submissive. My family wasn't comfortable with my behavior because of the machismo Latin culture.

While navigating the difficult family situation, Angel faced even more trouble at school:

> My Catholic school environment was a deeply traumatizing place, full of misogyny and homophobia, transphobia, and racism. A lot of the students were white, and students of color faced the harshest discipline. For me, it was even worse because of how I looked and acted.

In high school, theater became a safe place for Angel to express feelings and accept a non-conformist identity: "By playing other characters, you can express who you really are." After graduating high school, Angel completed a bachelor's degree in Theater at the University of Miami and went on to earn a Ph.D.

Helping Students Find Their Identity

However, Angel knew that identity meant the freedom to be one's full self, safely in all environments, especially in this particular high school where bullying had been a longstanding problem.

To address these issues, Angel's theater class put on a show for the entire high school and invited the parents. The production featured several LGBTQ+ lead characters who dated people of other races and religions, and students who preferred going into trades rather than on to higher education. Angel said, "We worked on short scenes that we developed out of students' experiences of being bullied at school, not being listened to by administrators, and feeling like they didn't have a voice in their own education."

The resulting show was highly interactive and seemed well-received. That is, until a small group of parents lodged a complaint with the school principal and with the theater department of the University of Miami. The parents accused Angel of inciting their children to turn away from Christian family values and of imposing unwelcome viewpoints on students. While the university expressed full support for Angel's teachings in response, the high-school principal called Angel in to discuss the protest and how best to move forward.

Angel recalled: "I was disappointed that parents felt the need to speak against the production. If they could see how much the students benefit from the safe, open space we create, they might feel differently." Angel also realized that positive interactions with the disgruntled parents would also help the students more honestly express themselves at home.

Resolving the Parents' Complaint

"The whole point of theater and live performance, I believe, is to get people talking and listening to each other," Angel said. "I guess we got people talking, and it's part of my job to listen to them and understand their point of view."

Handling the parents' complaints would require careful next steps. "I want to make sure I can continue helping students express themselves and see this as a teachable moment for everyone. The question is how to make the most of it."

Questions to Consider

Put yourself in Angel's shoes and think about the challenges ahead as you consider the following questions.

1. What are the viewpoints of the different stakeholders: Angel, the students, the university, the high-school leadership, and the parents who lodged the complaint? Where are the points of misalignment and conflict?
2. What would you include in your plan to address the parents' complaint at the high school? What statements would you make to the parents, what changes to the theater curriculum, and what explanations about the conflict would you give to the students?
3. How would this affect your future teaching and theater efforts, if at all?
4. Now, think of your own identity/life situation as you consider the following questions:

    • What aspects of your identity do you "leave at the door" at school, work, home, with friends, with colleagues, with family? How does that impact your effectiveness and comfort in various situations? What are the risks of being fully yourself?
    • Who defines your identity in different circumstances and sets the rules for what kind of expression is permissible? What are the sources of conflict or misalignment related to this process?
    • How can you and those around you—classmates, colleagues, and others—create a safe environment that encourages sharing of one's "whole self?" What outside resources, such as psychologists and diversity experts, might be able to help?

Notes

1 Susanne Mentzer, quote from *The Eternal Feminine*, CD liner notes, KOCH International 2001.
2 *The Eternal Feminine* radio program, broadcast on WFMT Radio Network, February 21, 2001.

3 Zarin Mehta, conversation with Ann Feldman, personal Day-timers Journal, May 17, 1999.

4 Libby Larsen, *The Eternal Feminine*, musical CD.

5 Sunny Fischer, *The Eternal Feminine*, radio program.

6 Liane Curtis, *The Eternal Feminine*, radio program.

7 Mentzer, *The Eternal Feminine*, CD, op.cit.

8 Larsen, *The Eternal Feminine*, radio program, op.cit.

9 YouTube link for streaming, www.amazon.com/Eternal-Feminine-Rutenberg-Susanne-Mentzer/dp/B073V47WDN. With permission from Entertainment One.

10 Larson, *The Eternal Feminine*, radio program, op.cit.

11 Dr. Judith Tick, interview with Ann Feldman, June 16, 2000.

12 John von Rhein, quote from "Ten Best Concerts of 2000," Arts Section cover, *Chicago Tribune*, printed in *The Eternal Feminine*, CD liner notes, KOCH International 2001.

13 Wynne Delacoma, music critic for the *Sun-Times*, August 2001, review of the concert.

References

1. National Endowment for the Arts. *A Decade of Arts Engagement: Findings from the Survey of Public Participation in the Arts, 2002–2012*. National Endowment for the Arts. https://www.arts.gov/sites/default/files/2012-sppa-feb2015.pdf.

2. O'Brien, Elena P. *The Meaning of the Eternal Feminine in Goethe's Faust*. Master's thesis, Florida State University Press, Tallahassee, FL, 2012.

3. De Beauvoir, Simone. "Chapter VI: Myth and Reality." In: *The Second Sex*. New York: Vintage, 1989.

4. Von Glahn, Denise. *Libby Larsen: Composing an American Life*. Urbana, IL: University of Illinois Press, 2017.

6 Connect

"Ties That Bind" Peace Project at 9/11: Connect to the Groups Most Affected by Conflict and Create Communities of Trust

> When disasters like 9/11 strike, you can work to build bridges with the most impacted groups. Find people in your community who are open-minded, compassionate, unafraid, and interested in repairing the world. Be patient and build locally to create national and international models. Use the power of media to keep everyone at the table—people want to be seen and heard. The right media can amplify your message.

Ties That Bind was a five-year peace project and video documentary created from the horrific events of 9/11. For this work, we brought together women religious leaders and their congregants from the Muslim, Jewish, Catholic, Latino Protestant, and Black Evangelical communities. Our documentary was broadcast nationally by the National Educational Telecommunications Associations (NETA) and internationally by John McLean Media.

Our accompanying discussion guide and video clips were used for educational outreach by the United Nations, PBS Learning Media, colleges and universities, and religious and secular organizations around the world. The documentary was nominated for an Emmy Award; won Chris, Accolade, and Aurora film awards; and was a finalist for the National Broadcast Society competition for video.

Along the way, we learned some important lessons for future projects such as this one:

- Understand that there is no road map during times of disaster. In many cases, you have to make it up as you go along.
- Listen to others, pivot, compromise, and change direction to suit the needs of your partners.

DOI: 10.4324/9781003296423-7

- Apply these lessons beyond the crisis to wider communities.
- Train youth to take on leadership roles.

Disaster Strikes the US—September 11, 2001

In a two-hour period on 9/11, Americans lost trust in their own safety. As the Pentagon was hit and the Twin Towers in New York City came down, so did our sense of protection and security. We were all connected to and affected by the disaster. The differences were in how we responded to the crisis.

Stage 1: Motivation

While friends and family were glued to the TV, watching the endless replays of the planes hitting the Twin Towers and their collapse and re-living the horrors of hundreds of innocent deaths, I was on the phone and at my computer, sending emails. An idea that had been percolating was ready to be born: I wanted to create a Festival of Women and Sacred Music.

Why? To provide love, beauty, and compassion as antidotes to the betrayal, anger, and fear that overcame our lives on September 11. The festival would be a way to counter the haunting images of death and destruction with music, spirituality, compassion, and hope. Despite the carnage and cruelty, I still believed in the power of connecting across barriers and building trust across diversity.

The women I contacted shared my worldview. I started with close friends—female religious leaders who had spent their lives, talents, and energies working to better the world. These women had gone beyond traditional women's roles and become leaders in their various religions— Catholicism, Protestantism, and Judaism. My first call was to Sister Kathy Sherman, a member of the Sisters of St. Joseph LaGrange. As a talented singer and songwriter, she had devoted her life to using the power of music to transform relationships among people of different nationalities, races, gender identities, and ethnicities.

Kathy and I both believed that music is the universal language. In her work teaching bilingual songs to Hispanic children, she said, "Music is a great bridge builder." I'd learned the same lesson in my decades as a cantorial and church soloist.

We brainstormed about an International Festival of Women and Sacred Music, but Kathy gently reminded me that this was not practical during a time of restricted travel and international distrust. In addition, the projected costs would be too high.

But we could start with local women religious leaders. Sister Pat Bergen, also a member of the Sisters of St. Joseph and an extraordinary counselor, joined our group, as did Rabbi Andrea London, from Beth Emet Synagogue in Evanston, IL. Rabbi London had worked hard to build relations between the Jewish synagogue and the Muslim community and had created initiatives for racial equity with Black leaders in Evanston.

The nuns, Rabbi London, Artistic Circles' board, and I decided to use our home base, Chicago, to advantage and focus on women religious leaders from the area as a way to create a community of trust. *Build Local* became our motto. We would bring together women religious leaders from the Catholic, Jewish, Black Evangelical, Latino Protestant, and Muslim traditions and their communities in interfaith conversations. Since female religious leaders were often "under the radar" in terms of formal acknowledgment within their communities and by their religious hierarchies, they could more easily join together in this time of distrust than could their more visible male counterparts.

To say it was difficult to arrange appointments or make inroads with Muslims would be an understatement. They were reeling after 9/11. Everyone was suspicious of them, and prejudices ran deep. Since Muslim women weren't given the title of Imam (the leading cleric), their female leaders were difficult to identify. Even when I found a Muslim female leader, other problems arose. Dr. Laleh Bakhtiar was a brilliant scholar and leader of women. However, she was also a Sufi, a sect of the Islamic religion that didn't attract a large national Muslim backing. Other Muslim female leaders told us that they couldn't participate due to restrictions about modesty and the Prophet's warnings about being humble.

I decided to pivot and instead approach female ministers in the Black Evangelical and Latino Protestant traditions. I met with Rev. Addie Wyatt, a union leader and co-parson with her husband of the Vernon Park Church of God. She wanted to pass down the lessons she learned in ministry and union activism to the younger generation. She brought in Rev. Willie Barrow, from Rainbow PUSH Coalition, someone who inspired us all. She was nicknamed "the Little Warrior" because of her small size and fierce energy for her work. As she proclaimed often:

> There is no Arab heart and there is no Jewish heart. And there is no African American heart. And once we really deal with that, we build connections, and we build unity. That's where we get our strength from to fight the daily fight.[1]

Then, I located Rev. Annie Gonzalez, a Methodist minister at San Lucas United Church of Christ, a bilingual community in Humboldt Park, IL. Annie also ran a program for women newly released from prison. She immediately joined us. Our efforts to connect with Muslim female leaders improved when I was introduced to the Council of Islamic Organizations of Greater Chicago (CIOGC). Their liaison, attorney Amina Saeed, was a brilliant woman with a talent for getting things done. She brought Muslim women doctors, lawyers, CPAs, educators, and artists into the project.

We now had female leaders from Chicago's main faiths—Muslim, Jewish, Catholic, Black Evangelical, and Latino Protestant. As a next step, I struggled to find the best format to capture their talents, charisma, energy, and good will. Radio couldn't portray the physical vibrancy and electric connections among them. The answer was to create a television documentary—an enormous undertaking that would require a major outlay of funds, time, and staff.

Stage 2: Get Everyone Together

We needed to bring all these women leaders together in one place and film their discussions and interactions. Funded by The Chicago Community Trust and Joyce Foundations, 50 women religious leaders agreed to gather on April 1, 2003, for lunch and conversations. Jan Thompson (my audio engineer from the China project) and her crew videotaped the event.

That day, we met at the South Shore Community Center, an historic building on Chicago's south side. We'd start the two-hour event with a storytelling session from Chicago's Black Evangelical, Latino, Jewish, Muslim, Lutheran, and Catholic leaders. We arranged a dozen tables, each one seating representatives from all the religious groups. After the individual presentations, there would be group discussions at each table, prompted by a set of questions and ideas. At the end of the day, we would ask the leaders to fill out a questionnaire with ideas about how to help create the documentary.

The room was charged with excitement and hope as the women leaders shared their dreams and concerns. After the introductions, one leader from each community stood up and presented her version of "How we can create social change despite the obstacles?"

Black Evangelical leader Rev. Addie Wyatt spoke of her advocacy for the unions and recited the words to the "Union Song." Leaning on a cane and with her shining face, she proudly encouraged all and stated, "We need to fall in love with each other!"

The love in the room was palpable.

Latino leader Rev. Annie Gonzalez coined the phrase that became our watchword, calling this a "Spiritual Map Quest: We all are on a Path. Each path may be different, but all of us are on a common path to the Divine."

Sister Kathy Sherman sang "One Voice," a song she'd written for the occasion and then taught to all of those assembled. I'd hoped this song would touch everyone and become a catalyst to bring people together. That wasn't meant to be. Instead, the fragile veneer of goodwill began to crack. The Muslims sat in stony silence, lips pressed together.

That undercurrent stirred some dark waters, made clear by the post-meeting feedback from people I trusted. A misunderstanding of one another's cultures led to a tone-deaf moment that could have shut down the entire project. The problem? Muslim leader Amina Saeed told me, "There is NO music in the mosque."[2]

And then, reactions to filming the day's event emerged. The April 1 video was a pivotal part of documenting the project and bringing it to the world, but there was a snag. One of the leaders refused to sign the permissions agreement that would allow her content to be included in our documentary. Since she was in each of the important interactions, the film was completely unusable. The hope and curiosity that brought us all together quickly faded. Trust had been broken.

Stage 3: Mistrust and Compromise

The strands of the six different communities had unraveled at our first event—one we'd hoped would knit them all together. Without realizing it, our assumptions about each other became judgmental. Christians and Jews believed that music was the universal language, unwittingly putting the Muslims in an awkward position. Also, the video crew, the Artistic Circles' board, and I had assumed that the leaders would be happy to be in the film. Instead, at least one leader feared we might misrepresent her.

The entire project was threatening to fall apart, and I no idea how to put it back together. I began by meeting with Amina Saeed and her Muslim colleagues to ask for their guidance. I apologized for our lack of sensitivity at the event and asked, "Are there any arts in Islam that Muslims could showcase instead of music?" That question helped transform their distrust into excitement as they told me about sacred calligraphy—writing quotes from the Qur'an or the word "Allah" as artwork for the inside of the mosques. We had a start.

Now that the conversation had become more open and honest, Amina mentioned another objection: "We can't participate in a project with the title 'Women and Sacred Music.'"

At first, I panicked. Then, I realized that we didn't need "music" in the title, especially when the Muslims were presenting calligraphy. I got creative and came up with a list of alternate titles. The Muslim women chose "Ties That Bind" (little realizing that it came from a famous Lutheran hymn "Ties That Bind").[3] The project was reborn.

The Muslim women had trusted us enough to tell us the truth, and together we learned to compromise. We expanded this model of compromise to give all the women leaders more control about filming in their diverse faith communities. We asked them "Why don't *you* choose what we'll film? That way you can speak for and represent yourselves."

A bumpy start to our peace project, but you can't expect to repair the world in three easy lessons.

Stage 4: Filming in the Neighborhoods

> "In the springtime, we filmed holidays that shared a common origin in Christianity and Judaism."
>
> Easter and Passover

The Easter service at Rev. Wyatt's Vernon Park Church of God on Chicago's south side was filled with ecstasy—people singing gospel music, raising hands in prayer, and sitting and being with family and friends in celebration.

As a counterpoint to the spectacular church Easter filming, we chose to film at a private home for the Jewish Passover seder. This ritual meal and service recounted the story of the Jews' experience as slaves in ancient Egypt and their fight for freedom. That longing for freedom was something we hoped all people could understand.

Each community had vibrant service programs. We filmed a soup kitchen at Beth Emet synagogue in Evanston and at the San Lucas United Church of Christ in Humboldt Park. For the homeless, those meals made the difference between life and death. We realized that any one of us, without good fortune, could easily be in their shoes.

Stage 5: Overcoming Biases

Another strand in the tapestry binding the women leaders together were obstacles they had to overcome to be recognized, trained, and taken seriously as women religious leaders.

Rev. Annie Gonzalez shared the story of her fight to follow her calling to be a minister: "I was in my twenties. I went to my minister, telling him I was being called to become a preacher. The minister laughed, saying, 'You must have heard it wrong.'" Annie ignored him, persevered, and answered her calling.

Sister Pat Bergen, of the Sisters of St. Joseph in LaGrange: "I knew I wanted to be a priest. I worked in a parish, and I began to realize that I could do more good for the people outside the parish structure. I love my work."[4] She became a spiritual counselor not only for other nuns but also to high-school students and male ministers.

By Thanksgiving, we had filmed in Black Evangelical, Jewish, Catholic and Latino Protestant communities. However, we still hadn't found a willing female Islamic religious leader. We had a strong partnership with secular Muslims and an esteemed Islam scholar on board, but no woman working day to day leading the Muslim women in prayer.

Then, through our Muslim board member, I learned about Aisheh Said, wife of the Imam at Bridgeview's large and well-known mosque. Aisheh was not only a respected scholar of Islam and a social worker but also led women in prayer. She would be a perfect addition to our team.

However, digging deeper, I discovered that the Bridgeview Mosque had a controversial history. The US Attorney General had indicted two of that mosque's members for running nonprofits with possible ties to Hamas, and there were intimations that the mosque's leadership might also be involved.[5],[6] Jewish friends and funders strongly advised me not to work with the Bridgeview Mosque. However, as a producer and an activist, I believed that Aisheh and the mosque were the right choice as our Muslim partners. Our board president, Potter Palmer, and the rest of the board agreed. We didn't let others' concerns and possible biases stop us. After all, this was a *peace* project.

I joined with Muslim interfaith leader Karen Danielson (a convert to Islam) to meet with Aisheh and her husband, the Imam. I made the case that Bridgeview and many Muslims suffered from a lack of control over stories

Figure 6.1 Female Muslim teacher reading Qur'an.

Source: Screenshot from *Ties That Bind* documentary. Photograph by the author

about them in the press. I asked them, "Why not tell your own story, of what it means to be a Muslim in America?"

At first, Aisheh modestly resisted being filmed, but her husband, the Imam, encouraged her, saying, "You'll get used to [the attention]." He understood the importance of Muslims representing themselves through the media.

Cameras rolled as Aisheh taught Qur'an classes to the women and children. We learned about her social work with the women, and she shared her heart-wrenching story, which had led to her current role as a leader:

> I was born in a refugee camp in Jordan. My parents left Palestine in 1948 and are Palestinian refugees. I was raised in the camp until I was six years old. I am a born social worker. It's part of me, the suffering, the feeling of others. It seems like I'm saying, I feel your pain.[7]

Aisheh showed great courage in trusting me, a Jew, to bring her into an interfaith project.

Stage 6: Facing Fear When Things Fall Apart

It can be terrifying to approach uncomfortable truths, but that's when you need to embrace your fear. It's a way to move forward and solve problems in partnership with your communities.

By December of 2003, we had excellent footage from each religious community. However, what was missing were vibrant interactions among the women leaders. I suggested a "girls' sleepover," where we could share meals, confide in one another, and tackle the difficult issues we all faced. Sisters of St. Joseph in LaGrange, IL offered to host us.

Once again, a filmed interfaith gathering brought out the best and worst in the participants. When secular Muslims from CIOGC learned that Palestinian Arab Aisheh Said would represent them, they backed out. That triggered a domino effect. The Evangelical leader refused to sign the agreement to film, expressing her earlier fear that her community's message would be misrepresented. A third leader had emergency back surgery.

Our retreat unraveled. We still hadn't captured the essence of the project—powerful exchanges *among* the women, a sense of sisterhood, common bonds, the ties that bind. I worried, Was our project dead? After much anguish, it finally dawned on me. Things had fallen apart before, and through compromise and good luck, we repaired them, making the relationships even stronger.

We held our ground. Despite objections from both the Muslim and Jewish communities, we stood behind Aisheh Said as the Muslim leader for our film. The leader who'd refused to sign the permission release for filming, now agreed to sign it. And the leader with back surgery healed. We decided to try again.

We rescheduled the retreat for March 4, 2004. On the first day, the leader who'd flip-flopped on the permission agreement once again didn't sign it and then never showed up. Another leader came an hour late, right in the middle of filming, and told us that she wouldn't stay past dinner. It was painful, but I had to turn her away.

That left eight brave souls who risked coming and staying together. We began with an exercise combining the threads of their different traditions, personalities, and communities. I took out a multi-colored ball of yarn, threw it to Sister Kathy, and yelled, "How will you connect with these women?" Kathy sang a song of peace, wrapped the end of the yarn around her wrist, then threw the ball of yarn to Annie, who, promptly dropped it, provoking a general, good-natured laughter.

The yarn flew back and forth among the women, weaving their stories, funny anecdotes, and serious messages into an elaborate design. The overall message was: "Define your own identities, spreading the good word of interfaith. Don't let the media do that for us. Say 'no' to violence."[8]

The strongest part of the day was our discussion of fears and stereotypes. The tension in the room echoed the topic. We weren't sure what to

Figure 6.2 Female religious leaders in a circle.
Source: Photograph by Eliza Levy for Artistic Circles

expect. While these women all agreed to speak honestly, that didn't mean we weren't afraid.

With butterflies in my stomach, I began by reading from a few 3 × 5 note cards I had:

> Which labels/stereotypes about yourself do you fear?
> Do you label or stereotype others?
> When there are hate crimes and violence, what is your response?[9]

The women's brutally honest answers revealed some surprises. Both Rabbi Andrea London and Muslim Karen Danielson shared their personal Israel/Palestine experiences during the Gulf War. Both felt like victims: Andrea was afraid to eat at a crowded restaurant for fear of it being bombed; Karen had been ostracized by soldiers who labelled her husband a possible terrorist. Then, Karen and Andrea looked at each other in wide-eyed shock, as they suddenly realized that they had both been in the same city in Israel/Palestine at the same time. *Ties That Bind.*

Rev. Barrow lamented the atmosphere of fear devouring both our country and the world and preached, "We are not so much divided, as we are disconnected. So, connect!"

"Connect" became our motto for Ties That Bind.

Later that night, we witnessed something extraordinary. Rabbi London and Aisheh Said sat together in the dining room with their open copies of the Torah and Qur'an side by side. They were debating points of law, finding common ground, and admitting differences. Rev. Barrow wisely whispered to me, "Let's leave them to it. Connections like these are at the heart of this project."

The following day, the women spent hours working to design a ritual that honored all their separate and collective beliefs. There could be no breaking of bread or drinking of wine because Muslims didn't imbibe. Lighting a candle and saying blessings had meaning for some groups but not for others. Rev. Annie wanted to honor her own Hispanic heritage and speak Spanish. The result was a compromise. They could all say the words, "I believe in peace and justice," in their own languages and through their own traditions. As they did so, the women held hands and formed a circle—the symbol for *Ties That Bind.*

Could Our Success Be a Model for Others?

We'd brought together eight important female religious leaders for dialogue, and we had filmed their different communities. The story was complete . . . or was it? Could we take the best elements of the retreat and inspire others to trust each other? Perhaps, those filmed conversations could serve as a roadmap for others to repair their own divided communities.

Going Public With Our Peace Project

The next 18 months became a series of presentations, town hall meetings, filming, and educational outreach. By the fall of 2004, we went to Barcelona, Spain, to show our documentary trailer at a "Pathways to Peace" conference put on by UNESCO and a Parliament of the World's Religions. After viewing the trailer, audiences asked some difficult questions:

> Why don't you include men?
> Why not include other religions?
> How influential are the women leaders' messages for regular people?
> What's next for this work?[10]

Using Our Work for Corporate Diversity

We'd created a model of trust among female religious leaders, and shown our work at a major international conference. Now, we wanted to use the documentary clips as conversation starters in other venues. Board president Potter Palmer suggested Exelon, the national electric company ComEd, where one of his colleagues was the CEO. Exelon had a corporate diversity program, but they struggled to get their various groups—Latinos, women, African Americans, LGBTQ, and Asians—to interact with one another and the White corporate management. We believed that, through filming conversations among their ethnic, gendered, and nationalistic groups, we could help infuse the model of *Ties That Bind* into this mainstream American corporate culture.

At first, the business executives were wary, but as soon as the novelty of our cameras wore off, their own authentic desires for equity and equality won out. They all had something to say. Those conversations had not happened before publicly at the corporate offices.

Instead of religion or faith, they focused on the workplace environment and found two major issues that stood out:

(1) The lack of interaction among the diverse groups. A possible solution? Why not plan a Diversity Gala at the corporation, sharing food from different cultures and learning about each other's cultural arts?
(2) Economic inequities made overcoming racial and ethnic prejudices more difficult. The diverse groups asked that White executives and

Figure 6.3 Corporate executives discuss diversity.
Source: Photograph by Nan Stein Photography LLC

managers be involved in these diversity conversations. Within a corporate structure, it took bravery to speak truth to power.[11]

Discussing such fears ignited dynamic, productive, and passionate conversations about race and economic inequality and how to resolve these problems in a corporate environment.

Using the Ties That Bind *Model in High Schools*

Our next step was to bring this project to high-school students at the Chicago Public Schools and to the National Council of Community and Justice (NCCJ). A group of diverse students sat together—16-year-old Latino, African American, Irish, and Italian youth—talking and trying to find solutions about their separated communities. One idea was to organize a "Mix It Up" day at their high school where they would break out of their regular pattern of sitting only with friends like themselves to meet new people. High school can be extremely polarizing, and there is a lot of pressure to fit in. Students have a universal need to belong. One girl spoke honestly about what scared her: "I am afraid of being singled out because I represent racial differences.

Figure 6.4 High-school students discuss race.

Source: Photograph by Nan Stein Photography LLC

In the high school lunchroom, sometimes if I move tables, I'm called *traitor, cracker, acting White/Black*."[12]

It hurts, and it's not easy for teenagers to give voice to their real feelings. A fragile dialogue began as the students shared honestly with one another— just as the women religious leaders and the groups at Exelon had done.

Educational Outreach

We needed an educational product that would take our team and Artistic Circles out of the equation and put diverse communities in charge of their own future conversations. That product became a discussion guide based on the core issues and strategies for social change identified by the participating communities.

The guide was divided into five general topics: Connections, Spiritual Expressions, Looking at Fears, Conversations, and Community Involvement. Each religious and secular group could add their own actions and ideas to identify their common issues, get to know one another, and form ties that bind them together. We used quotes and photographs from earlier community gatherings to serve as models for the work.

The most valuable section of the discussion booklet was "Do It Yourself Outreach." This was a how-to guide to help create your own town-hall meeting. Each booklet came with 20 minutes of video clips from our documentary to help spark the discussions and model how to cross boundaries. The tapestry of inclusion wove together groups of people across economic, racial, ethnic, gendered, religious, and political boundaries.

Let It Go: The Media and *Ties That Bind*

On September 11, 2006—five years after 9/11—the *Ties That Bind* peace documentary was broadcast across the US and around the world. The National Educational Telecommunications Association (NETA) aired *Ties That Bind* on national public television stations, and John McLean Media syndicated it internationally. The accompanying discussion guide with video clips was sent across the country and around the world as well. It was used by PBS Learning Media and the United Nations and adopted by colleges, universities, and high schools nationally and internationally.

Ties That Bind won an Emmy nomination and film awards from Accolade and Aurora. I also received a Friendship Award from the Bridgeview Mosque, one of the most joyous experiences for me of this project. Another proud moment was when the men of the Muslim American Society (MAS) partnered with public TV stations around the country to hold town-hall meetings in 22 cities in conjunction with our broadcast.

Reunion of Women Leaders

Thirteen years later in 2019, I'd lost touch with many of the women religious leaders, and they barely kept in contact with each other. The daily pressures of feeding the hungry, counseling their congregants, weddings and funerals, weekly services, and teachings kept them very busy.

I decided to plan a reunion of all the leaders in Chicago in fall 2019.[13] The only one who wouldn't be there was Rev. Willie Barrow, the Little Warrior, who had passed away. We dedicated our reunion to her, focusing on her life's message: "We're not so divided as we are disconnected. So, *let's connect.*"

The leaders were worn out, all trying to balance the needs of their communities with their interfaith work. The Muslim leader, Karen Danielson, devised a solution: training the younger generation to take over the work of interfaith and intercommunity connections. Together with her students at the girls' Muslim school, we could begin that process at a retreat there the following year.

For the retreat, Sister Kathy Sherman coined the phrase "inter-community" rather than interfaith. Two undergraduate interns from Northwestern University, Eliza Levy and Amy Rogin, joined us for the retreat and encouraged the leaders to move beyond "Us versus Them, the Right way and the Wrong way." They said that young people might not participate from a religious standpoint but rather from their own common social and civic goals.[14]

Final Thoughts

Trying to create *Ties That Bind* after the 9/11 disaster was like walking on quicksand. We constantly had to re-balance, change directions, and ask for help. Over a period of five years, from 2001 to 2006, hundreds of participants took the risk to reach out to strangers, host them in their communities, discuss difficult ideas, fail, and ultimately succeed. While there was little solid ground under us in creating this peace project, there was good will and the promise of a better future.

The interfaith, inter-community conversations in the film belong to everyone. All of us are potential role models in the struggle to make the world a kinder and better place, especially young people. The risks involved are worth taking, giving us all a reason to hope.

Chapter 6 Case Study: Forging Connections

Alissa Roman wanted to connect with individuals and groups from different backgrounds and situations than hers but wasn't sure how best to do that.

The 21 year old, a senior at Northwestern University, joined a social-impact program through which students could volunteer to help prison inmates improve their writing skills—for employment as well as creative pursuits such as memoir-writing. "I want my career to be about empowering the poor and overlooked," Alissa said. "I want to channel my passion for social justice into meaningful work."

She arrived at the prison facility excited to work toward making a difference. But in the first session, things didn't go quite as expected: the five to six inmates she was assigned for small-group lessons were polite but seemed distant and uninterested, despite having volunteered for the class. When she tried to engage them in planned writing exercises, they were dismissive. Their informal leader, Wardell, openly questioned the value of the program: "Lots of us are in here for years more, so what's the point of getting better at writing? What can a girl teach us?"

Alissa took the comments to heart. She met with the directors of the program to get advice. They discussed the demographic gap and explained: "Many of the prisoners suspect strangers, and for good reason—society hadn't treated them well. As a young White female stepping into a classroom full of older men, primarily men of color, you need to earn their trust."

A Way Forward?

As a young White female, Alissa knew she was at a disadvantage in the prison setting. So, she approached an older Northwestern student who'd volunteered for the program for two years and received helpful advice: "Find the leader in the group and ask him what he wants from the class. Be willing to show him and the group that you don't come with all the answers."

Alissa identified Wardell as the leader, but knew that he was skeptical of her and the writing program. She began the second class with a disclaimer: "I know that most of you don't trust me, for good reason. You don't know me, and I don't know you. But I want to get to know you and help you become better writers." Then she turned to Wardell. "What do *you* want to write?"

Wardell was surprised. "I want to write a letter to my son. But there's so much to say, and I need the right words." Alissa was glad to find an opening. "The words aren't as important as showing your son you care," she said. "That's the core of any meaningful writing."

Wardell looked at the other inmates, cleared his throat, and said,

> My son Ronald is really important to me. He'll be 19 next week, and I worry about him a lot. He has cerebral palsy and can't really have the kind of life I would want for him. But I'm in here, so it feels like there's not much I can do for him.

Alissa was touched by Wardell's disclosure and now saw a way forward to better engagement. She thought about how best to respond to Wardell's desire in a way that would galvanize the group around the program's mission and encourage them to share their own hopes, dreams, and concerns through written and spoken communication.

Alissa considered telling her own story, which included helping a younger sister with cognitive disabilities. That might provide a connection to Wardell and the others. "Empathy is critical in any community-service effort," she said, "But I wanted to be careful not to shift the group's focus to me." She thought about how to forge an ongoing connection with the group where both sides could benefit.

Questions to Consider

If you were in Alissa's shoes, how would you approach forging a connection to her class?

1. What factors might create a "You versus Us" environment in this case study? What labels or stereotypes might each side have of the other? What actions or steps might transform "You versus Us" into "We?"
2. Would you encourage Alissa to share the story of her sister with the group? Why or why not? If you think she should, what might be the best way to do so?
3. How can Alissa forge a deeper connection with the group, building off the opportunity Wardell presented?
4. How could Alissa's experience help shape your thinking about community, opportunity, and social justice and different ways to address injustice?
5. Think about a diverse community you want to connect with that may be different from your own. What separates you from the group? What common goals or experiences do you and that community share? How can you use this common ground to form connections?
6. Do you know people who can connect diverse groups and are successful agents of change? What influence do they have? What can you learn from them?

Notes

1 Rev. Willie Barrow. Statement made during the taping of the women's retreat for *Ties That Bind* in April 2004.
2 Ann Feldman's Journal, January 1, 2003–August 16, 2003, April 1, 2003 event.
3 John Fawcettt. *Blessed Be the Ties That Bind*, lyrics, 1782, https://hymnary.org/text/blest_be_the_tie_that_binds.
4 Sister Pat Bergen. Leaders' section of Artistic Circles' Discussion Guide about *Ties That Bind*, Artistic Circles, 2006, 5.
5 *Terrorism Awareness Project*, a periodic newsletter updating the Chicago Connection to International Terrorism, the Jewish Community Relations Council of the Jewish United Fund of Metropolitan Chicago, May 2003, Vol. 1, No. 1.
6 Jacob Parzen. Illinois Islamic Radicalization Index, ICT, International Institute for Counter-Terrorism, July 30, 2012.
7 Artistic Circles' booklet, op.cit., p. 11.
8 *Ties That Bind*, video documentary, September 11, 2006. NETA (National Educational Telecommunications Association) in the U.S., and John McLean Media internationally.
9 *Ties That Bind*, discussion guide, p. 9.
10 "Pathways to Peace" conference in Barcelona, Spain, July 8, 2004.
11 *Ties That Bind*, discussion guide, op.cit., pp. 12, 25.

12 Ibid., p. 12.
13 *Ties That Bind*, website for Artistic Circles, 2019 Reunion, www.waterpressures.org/copy-of-ties-that-bind.
14 Many of the photographs are stills captured from the Ties That Bind documentary.

References

1. Marty, Martin. *Being Good and Doing Good*. Minneapolis, MN: Fortress Press, 1984; Marty, Martin and Jonathan Moore. *Education, Religion and the Common Good: Advancing a Distinctly American Conversation About Religion's Role in Our Shared Life*. San Francisco: Jossey-Bass, 2000; Marty, Martin and Jonathan Moore. *When Faiths Collide*. Oxford: Blackwell, 2005.
2. Mattson, Ingrid. "Chapter 4: Gender and Sexuality in Islamic Bioethics." In Alirezi Bagheri, ed., *Islamic Bioethics: Current Issues and Challenges*. World Scientific Publishing Europe, Ltd., Vol. 2, 57–84. https://ingridmattson.org/wp-content/uploads/2020/06/Mattson-Ingrid-Gender-and-Sexuality-in-Islamic-Bioethics.pdf.
3. Patel, Eboo. *Interfaith Leadership*. Boston, MA: Beacon Press, 2016.

7 Water Hierarchy

"Water Pressures": Use the Power of Partnerships to Address Local and Global Water Issues

Academia can take a leading role in working globally for safe water. In these efforts, it's important to include stakeholders from other industries as well, including NGOs, corporations, governments, villagers, celebrities, and media.

To address universal water issues. The only sustainable relationship among these groups is partnership. Creative projects such as video documentaries can bring together communities divided by thousands of miles and by economic and nationalistic differences. Solving water issues is the future of young people.

As the world warms, access to clean water becomes more and more imperative. The video documentary *Water Pressures* was the result of a partnership about water sustainability, formed between a desert community in Rajasthan, India, and students and faculty at Northwestern University in Evanston, IL. *Water Pressures* was broadcast on Earth Day, April 22, 2013, and was syndicated nationally by American Public Television and internationally by John McLean Media and Alexander Press.

In collaboration with a dozen organizations worldwide, a discussion guide accompanied the documentary and video clips for educational outreach. The United Nations and PBS Learning Media also used these materials in the US and abroad. The *Water Pressures* TV documentary won film awards from Accolade, Indie Fest, Green Unplugged, and the Chicago South Asian Film Festival.

Water for Life: Bangalore, India (February 2007)

We were headed to the airport, leaving India for Chicago, IL, when the stench of burning buildings reached me even in our cab. A chaotic scene

DOI: 10.4324/9781003296423-8

Figure 7.1 India water riot.
Source: Photograph by VP Praveen Kumar © Shutterstock

unfolded in front of us. The busy, four-lane highway was blocked with abandoned vehicles, and in the streets on either side, ill-clad looters darted in and out of charred shops. Thousands of riot police brandished their clubs but stayed on the sidelines of the melee.

I was shaking in my seat, but my traveling companion, Tibetan Buddhist monk Geshe Gendun Gyatso Konchhok, calmly explained this was a water riot. Impoverished villagers were protesting a recent court decision about water rights to the nearby Cauvery River. Once again, the wealthy and powerful would get the main rights, and poor farmers would be left with the dregs.

At first, I couldn't understand how water rights could trigger such violence. Growing up in Chicago, I was used to the endless supply of clean water from Lake Michigan. News reports of drought in the southwestern US, in India, and in Africa meant little to me.

Witnessing this riot made me realize that water was not just other people's problem but mine as well. Obviously, India had a great deal to teach me about this most precious shared commodity. Shaken out of my "water blindness," I felt compelled to do something. But what exactly?

On the flight back to Chicago, I evaluated my talents and networks. Artistic Circles had an 18-year history of creating media for social change. What if we could produce a documentary highlighting the global water crisis?

I had no idea that the project would take several trips to India and six years to complete.

Stage 1: Building Water Awareness at Home (Spring 2007)

Once back in Chicago, I met with my board of directors, and we decided to focus on building partnerships between radically different communities—rich/poor, powerful/powerless, and haves/have-nots—regarding the essential key to life on Earth, water.

However, before we could act globally, I needed to start at home with my own students and colleagues at Northwestern University in Evanston, IL, where I was teaching. I wanted to impress upon students that with overpopulation and global warming, water scarcity would be their future. Projections showed that by 2025, 1.8 billion people would be living in countries or regions with water scarcity, and two-thirds of the world's population could be living under water stressed conditions.[1]

Yet Evanston and Northwestern University were located on the shores of Lake Michigan, an abundant water source. How could we educate and galvanize college students about a global water crisis that didn't seem to touch them? I searched for partners on campus. Professor Yael Wolinsky was the Director of Environmental Studies. A desert native from Israel, she knew only too well about water scarcity and was an engaged teacher.

On campus, we began working on a "water awareness campaign" with interested Northwestern students. They learned how the casual, every-day choices made by Americans deeply impacted the water resources of other countries (especially developing countries). Northwestern students mounted a campaign to encourage other students to change their behavior, such as not buying new jeans, which require a large amount of water to manufacture in poorer countries. One student even circulated a petition on several campuses, hoping to obtain 100,000 signatures regarding the new jeans boycott from college students nationwide.

Stage 2: Partnering With India's Jal Bhagirathi Foundation

However, these efforts, though commendable, were far removed from the people who lived where water shortages were a constant fact of life. I decided that it was time to go back to India—but where in India?

Board member Katherine Bateman had a son, Lindsey Powell, who was working on a documentary film was about Maharaja Gaj Singh. In 2002, the Maharaja had founded the Jal Bhagirathi Foundation (JBF) in the Rajasthan Thar Desert to expand clean water sources for his villagers. Lindsey interceded on our behalf; and the Maharaja, who trusted Lindsey, granted us the opportunity to pitch the idea of a water documentary based on an East/West partnership.

JBF was a hands-on educational center where engineers were trained to work with villagers on rainwater catchment and where local nurses learned the most effective ways to educate people about contaminated water and water-borne diseases. The engineers and nurses lived in the community, often staying in the desert with the villagers and learning about their daily lives, concerns, and challenges.

I explained to the Maharaja that the message I wanted to share through film was that Indian water-distressed communities had a lot to teach Westerners, whose history of water waste was legendary. Indians didn't waste a drop of water and harvested and hauled it with respect. I learned that the people were wary of outsiders, especially corporations, who came in, tried a quick "technical fix," and left just as quickly.

The Maharaja explained that the villagers and their families had lived in the same thatched huts for generations, experienced dry seasons and monsoons, and had devised local, simple, and effective conservation techniques that worked. Their story was an important one for Westerners to hear.

Maybe, I suggested that Indians and Americans could work together to stop waste and to conserve and protect precious water resources locally and globally.

Stage 3: Building Trust in India (Spring 2008)

In Spring 2008, my Buddhist friend, Geshe, and I traveled to Jodhpur, India, to meet with JBF. Why did I include Geshe instead of a water or film expert? Primarily because he spoke Hindi, but more importantly, people trusted this religious leader. And, because Geshe and I were close friends, I could rely on him to tell me the truth of how the administrators, Maharaja, engineers, nurses, and villagers responded to me and my documentary idea. Geshe told me the clues he observed in the language, gestures, and behaviors of our hosts and the people we met. In building trust across boundaries, it's critical to surround yourself with truth-tellers.

Kanupriya Harish, the Executive Director of JBF, was the first person I met in Jodhpur. This young woman ran the operation on a day-to-day basis. She was intelligent, organized, and, like so many others, wary of our motives. Lots of organizations sent students to study at JBF, gave donations, or wanted to partner. She wanted to know: "What is different about your project and participants?"

I thought long and hard before answering. For nearly 20 years, I'd witnessed the power of media to create positive social change. If JBF wanted to spread their message of localized, community-based water conservation, then film was a strong vehicle.

But my personal motivation was different: I wanted to use media to bring together different communities who all had a stake in water—villagers, dignitaries, corporations, government officials, video artists, and academics. I'd learned that when cameras were present, diverse groups stayed together, tried harder to get along, and took more risks. This was partly because they knew we'd showcase them speaking for themselves and presenting their own points of view.

Kanupriya agreed to work with us and showed me documents about their programs, explaining how JBF partnered with the villagers. Then, she took us into the field, which was thrilling. Kanupriya, two engineers, Geshe, and I traveled in an open-air jeep, with scarfs tied over our noses and mouths to keep out the penetrating dust. As we drove deeper into the Thar Desert, we saw vast expanses of land without the slightest bit of water. All the *talabs* (ponds) were dry. The western part of the desert received only four inches of water a year; in Chicago, the average was 37 inches.

Stage 4: The Hard Reality of Women and Water

When we asked how the people got water for drinking, cooking, bathing, and cleaning here, I was shocked and dismayed by the answer.

The major burden of fetching and using water lay almost entirely on the slim shoulders of the women. They walked eight to ten hours a day deep into the desert to find and bring back the water, balancing two metal jugs on their heads and tucking two others under their arms, often with a baby strapped to their backs. They conserved every drop of precious water for cooking and cleaning. When they made these arduous walks, they wore open-toed sandals and had no hats or sunglasses. They simply couldn't afford them.

But that wasn't the only burden women faced. Once they reached puberty, they couldn't remain in school as there were no toilets where they could address issues of menstruation. It was clear that without water, men and especially women remained in an endless cycle of low education and poverty.

Yet even in the midst of all that sadness, something miraculous happened during our visit to the villagers. It rained! We even saw a few big black umbrellas come out. The women attributed the rains to me, the White woman from far away. Since I was a woman leading men and spearheading the documentary, they began to trust me as a vehicle to present their own needs and desires. The sari-covered desert women were confident that I would listen to and represent them fairly, and I promised them I would.

At the end of our visit, Kanupriya invited us to return to India with a film crew to document JBF's work for TV audiences—a story the world needed to hear. I agreed, but first, I had to develop the entire story we would tell. All I knew at present was that it would be based on partnerships between East (India) and West (US).

Figure 7.2. Indian woman carrying water pot on her head.
Source: Photograph by James Ward Ewing

Stage 5: Putting the Story Together (April and May 2008)

Once back at Northwestern, I analyzed the story I had so far:

- Most Americans were the "water haves." For instances, the Great Lakes held 26 percent of the world's freshwater. In contrast, the Thar Desert villagers in Rajasthan were "water have-nots."

- Water scarcity led to a downward spiral into poverty. Without access to clean water, children couldn't stay in school, become educated, and get decent-paying jobs.
- The burden of fetching, using, and conserving water fell primarily on women.
- Around the world, 780 million people didn't have access to improved water sources, and 2.5 billion lacked access to improved sanitation. An estimated 801,000 children younger than five years of age perished from diarrhea each year, mostly in developing countries.[2]

I brought these issues to my student interns at Northwestern. All were bright, caring problem-solvers. Emily Goligoski, a journalism major, launched a social media campaign to share the stories of water inequity: "As young adults build and share social technologies and mobile applications faster than ever before, it's crucial that they be the ones to ignite change around the issue of water depletion." She felt strongly that previous generations hadn't done enough about water sustainability and that now it was the responsibility of young people to be the leaders.

Other Northwestern professors saw an opportunity for their students to get involved and eagerly joined us. Professor Yael Wolinsky from Northwestern's Environmental Studies invited us to film her class as they held discussions about water issues. One young man admitted to taking 15-minute showers, letting the fresh, clean water run while he brushed his teeth, and admitted he bought new, water-unfriendly jeans. He hadn't known how his actions impacted others who lived so far away.

When I told the students about the water shortages in the Thar Desert, some were shocked. Others who had lived in the Southwest knew the problem first hand. But all the students asked, "What can we do? We can't transport excess water all the way to India." With Professor Wolinsky's prodding, they began the process of "acting locally and thinking globally."

Wolinksy and with her students devised a campus challenge to conserve water: turn off the faucets while brushing teeth, take shorter showers, and install low-flow shower heads and toilets. Engineering students from Design for America came up with creative solutions to use less water while washing dishes in the university's dining rooms. We filmed the students, as they were kayaking on Lake Michigan, studying the importance of Chicago as a port city where cargo boats docked with goods.

All of this was a story of abundance, the Western story. Now, we needed to show the other side of the story—scarcity, the Eastern story. I wanted the Indian villagers, engineers, healthcare workers, and water activists to speak for themselves. Then, to inspire change, we could take those stories back to Evanston and set up a full-blown water campaign.

But to make this dream happen, we needed partners and funders who knew and cared about India. We started with individuals and organizations that were India-based and knew the problems first hand. We spoke with Air India, India Development Coalition of America (IDCA), Tata Foundation, and the Sehgal Foundation, all led by South Asian Indians and with projects in India. I was gratified when they gave us their support.

Non-Asians also lent their support. Filmmaker Jan Thompson, who produced *Hidden India*, agreed to direct the filming in Rajasthan and take along two students as assistants. Photographer and cameraman James Ewing added his extraordinary talents to our crew.

Stage 6: Filming the Story in India (October 2008)

We needed a core idea to dramatically show the water scarcity and everyday challenges for villagers in the Thar Desert. Jan chose the image of a grade school filled with boys *and* girls—a shining story from JBF. Why? Because in partnership with JBF, the villagers had dug a well for fresh water, kept it clean for use by students and teachers, and built toilets. With toilets, the girls could stay in school as they reached puberty and started to menstruate.

A simple idea: In America, every parent took for granted that their kids would have access to running water and toilets at school. Not so in India. From this concept, the title of the documentary emerged: *Water Pressures*.

We then filmed what could happen when a community *didn't* have access to clean water and toilets. A 93-year-old woman told of a lifetime of days searching for water in the desert. Because there was no easy clean source and no toilets at the school near her, no one in her family could stay in school. That was how water scarcity led to an endless cycle of poverty.

Finally, we filmed what happened when well-intentioned Western corporations came to help. One company brought in desalination equipment to take the excess salt out of the groundwater. Unfortunately, the equipment kept breaking down due to extreme heat and sand. While the equipment did remove excess salt from groundwater, the salt was left on the ground and seeped back into the groundwater, making it undrinkable.

After this failed engineering project, the villagers learned to rely on and trust age-old local solutions that were more sustainable. These included harvesting rainwater from house roofs by using drainpipe catchments and expanding the size of the ponds to capture and hold rainwater during the monsoons—simple, cheap, and effective methods.

But rainwater catchment and conservation were small fixes. The bigger problem was to show the vast differences in basic water resources, such as those in Lake Michigan and the Thar Desert: Plenty versus Scarcity.

One personal note: As I managed the filming project, the villagers didn't know what to make of me. I was a woman but dressed more like a man with my short hair and khaki slacks and top. Even more remarkable, I was in charge of an all-male crew and gave them orders, which they followed! This was something the villagers had never seen from a Westerner. The women decided that I needed a "spa" day and gave me a manicure, complete with bright nail polish, and measured me for a sari. After that, I at least had something they recognized as feminine.

Stage 7: Alliances With Corporations/Government (2008–2010)

We needed bigger, more powerful corporate and government partners to invest in our project. It was partly one way that they could counter their own images of over-using Indian water sources and partly as a way to scale up clean-water efforts and help more people.

That's when I learned about an international alliance of corporations that was intent on minimizing their global water footprints. With the last $5,000 in Artistic Circles' bank account, I attended an International Corporate Water Foot-printing Conference in San Francisco, an insider meeting of the top corporations that were the biggest water users—Intel (computer chips), John Deere (agriculture), Miller Coors (beer), and PepsiCo and Coca-Cola (soft drinks).

Fortunately, they also had a small exhibition hall, and I set up a display about *Water Pressures*, showing colorful posters of the women in saris, the expanse of desert, and camels beside small ponds of water.

During the breaks, our booth attracted the attention of Dan Bena, Director of Sustainability at PepsiCo. As he explained later:

> There are certain people with whom there is an immediate human connection, even the very first time you meet. That's what happened when I first met Ann Feldman. . . . I somehow knew immediately – viscerally, not intellectually – that Ann was a human being of conscience, of values, and of passion. The years since that meeting have proven my initial feeling correct.[3]

Both PepsiCo and another corporation offered sponsorship for the project. When I brought these two options to JBF, they told me that they trusted PepsiCo. The company not only had a South Asian CEO, Indra Nooyi, but also had a good reputation of building wells in India and not depleting the water. However, JBF refused to work with the other corporation, which had used so much local water to produce their projects that the regional Indian governments sued them. PepsiCo became our premiere sponsor for *Water*

Pressures. We are indebted to Tim Carey, the present Chief Sustainability Officer, at PepsiCo for his support and partnership.

That initial success spurred me to search for other corporations and government officials that also cared about global water equity. I used two "hooks" to interest them: India itself and the young people of the world. Many corporations did business in India and knew that young people were the future of their companies.

We set up campus events to bring students, corporations, and government officials together around the topic of water scarcity and conservation. IBM's Vice President Valinda Scarbro Kennedy encouraged Northwestern students to apply for grants from "Students for a Smarter Planet" for their engineering and social change projects on campus.

Illinois Congresswoman Jan Schakowsky talked with the students to encourage advocacy for water and for political change. As she said:

> Sixty-three million Americans don't have access to safe drinking water. The kids are leading the way now and not waiting anymore for grown-ups and policy makers to get it done, and they're pretty fierce. We want that [passion] to be translated into votes, because the House of Representatives passes these bills, and Mitch McConnell, he's the Grim Reaper. Everything we pass is "dead on arrival" when it comes to the Senate. The politics of water can be weaponized for control.[4]

Congresswoman Schakowsky helped us understand that by empowering young people to vote, they could determine their *own* water futures. Corporations, government, media, academia, and water organizations from the US and India could became partners for *Water Pressures*. Trust was a two-way street and benefitted all the parties.

Now, the challenge was to bring the varied stakeholders face to face.

Stage 9: Exchange of East and West (April 2010)

Working with Prithivi Raj Singh, JBF's CEO, we came up with an exchange program: Northwestern students would go to Rajasthan to learn about water scarcity firsthand, and leaders from JBF would come to the US to witness our water abundance and to advocate for water equity. We'd film the exchanges to show Americans and international audiences what could be achieved through global water partnerships. The United Nations Development Programme (UNDP) funded the exchange. Northwestern appointed me as the Field Director, responsible for the students during a Study Abroad Program.

In total, eight students signed up for the Spring Break trip to Rajasthan in April 2010. They came from several disciplines: environmental studies,

Figure 7.3 Northwestern University students in India.

Source: Photograph by James Ward Ewing

engineering, pre-medicine, journalism, and political science. I went a week early to Rajasthan to make sure that all the arrangements were in place before the students and new film crew arrived. The plan had been that JBF would hold classes for the students about water scarcity, and the students would create a final project to help with the problem.

But in the time it took me to fly to India, the plans changed. From Prithvi's point of view, my idea wasn't what JBF wanted to happen:

> Ann was looking for some kind of an output from the students, like they would arrive, and we were going to be able to solve some problems. I told Ann that what I intend to do is put the students in different villages, and they stay there for three, four days or something like that, and we will leave them alone in the village and not as a group, as a single student in each village.[5]

Deeply disappointed by this unexpected turn, I asked Prithvi why the change in plans? He told me, "Because the students don't speak the local language, know the customs, or live here." JBF had worked for decades with engineers and nurses living with villagers to learn how best to address the local problems. A group of "green" students spending one week here wasn't going to solve a local problem that still challenged local experts.

Despite my misgivings, I realized that Prithvi was correct and that his plan was brilliant. Western arrogance had led me to think that we could arrive and, with good intentions, try to solve Eastern problems. After I settled down, talked with Geshe and Northwestern's administration, we agreed that this alternative plan was a great gift for the students, offering them an opportunity to walk in someone else's shoes. Our initial distrust turned into faith and reliance on our Indian hosts to see things through their worldview, not ours.

Most students had wonderful experiences. One student lived with a goatherd and learned to appreciate the utter quiet and restfulness of sitting for a day with nothing else to do. But not everything was as serious or contemplative. Suzanne, a political science major, stayed with a mother and her two daughters at a home with some wealth—a cow and the village's only toilet (unused, since the villagers were afraid of demons in the water). The family had a mischievous sense of humor and decided to play pranks on Suzanne—locking her in the toilet, telling her to pet the tame cow (it wasn't), and serving a memorable meal of super-spicy food.

However, two of the young men, Mert and Yuri, rebelled against living in the desert and letting the villagers lead them. They wanted to do something on their own and left the program to explore the area. This not only caused a rift in the fragile community we were creating between East and West but raised fears among the villagers, government officials, and Northwestern officials for the students' safety. Thar Desert was near the border with Pakistan, and there was a military camp not far away. Engineering student Yuri explained their thinking at the time:

> Mert and I were a couple years into the founding of our own organization, Design for America, and felt very strongly that there were lessons to be learned from the work that Bunker Roy was doing at the [nearby] Barefoot College. We just couldn't pass up the chance to see the place in person, being a short drive away. In retrospect, we were arrogant and fairly oblivious in those years, and I must admit that I cringe when I think back on the commotion we caused.[6]

Unfortunately, the two students' disregard for the East/West process unsettled the other students and deeply hurt our Indian hosts. (See video clip East-West Conflict which includes interviews with the students and host https://vimeo.com/manage/videos/60866904—password: water2012.)

Stage 10: Drawing on Trust to Save the Project

What kept the project from entirely derailing? The trust among JBF's leaders, engineers and villagers we had built over three years, the cool heads among us, and the decision not to escalate the situation. Kanupriya didn't bring this issue to her board. I didn't follow the advice of the Northwestern administrator to send the two young men back to the US with a black mark on their records. Together, we all managed to salvage the project.

For most of the students, their experiences of staying in the desert communities were the highlight of their trip. They refused to follow Mert and Yuri. For them, experiential learning was more valuable than trying to make a "contribution" without fully understanding the culture. Even Mert and Yuri learned something from their time in India. Since the Rajasthan trip, both of them have devoted their talents and passion to working on environmental issues.

For the Northwestern girls, the trust my crew and I had built up among the villagers brought some unexpected results during the two days in the villages. The girls and I shadowed some of the local women, trying to carry pots filled with water on our heads. None of us could handle the weight of 40 kilos (88 lbs.) on our necks or shoulders. The pots slid right off our heads. One of the girls complained that carrying the water was painful even on her hips—and that was only after five minutes of carrying water! The village women laughed good-naturedly at our ineptitude. However, the experience made a deep impression on me.

As I began watching the village women more closely, I noticed that they hobbled and winced as they walked. I could see that their sandaled feet had knobs and bunions more typical of grandmothers than of young women.

The pain I observed in the women's posture and pattern of walking was also evident in my overnight host, a young woman in her mid-20s. Her feet also had bunions and callouses and were swollen from having to bear such heavy weights. At one point, she took a break from her chores and led me upstairs to the roof. There the air was sweet, not like the smoke-filled kitchen where she spent most of her time. One of the cooking fuels they used was pungent cow dung.

Hoping to help ease some of her exhaustion, I decided to offer her a relaxing and healing foot rub. I motioned for her to sit, which she did. Then, I gestured for her to remove her sandals and showed her that I wanted to rub her feet. I had been trained in foot reflexology and knew from personal experience how healing a foot massage could be.

At first, she refused, but I insisted until she finally agreed. The moment I began rubbing her feet, she closed her eyes, moaned in relief, and relaxed. The pain reflected in her face lessened. Even at 22, she had likely carried the heavy water containers for over a decade, helping her mother and grandmother. The wear and tear on her young body showed.

The experience was deeply moving. To touch a stranger in another culture, especially something as intimate as the feet, was a great gift to us both and helped us connect on a deep level.

When the Northwestern students and I got back to JBF the next day, I mentioned that "foot" experience to Trustee Prithvi Raj Singh. I also told him about my concerns for the skeletal damage and general health of the women who carried such heavy water loads for so many years.

My unsolicited information set in motion some important changes for the women. Prithvi explained:

> I remembered what you said, and I shared it with some group of doctors who had come from some of the premiere medical institutions in India, and they had come to do research. "Why don't you look at the skeleton of a woman who is carrying something like 40 kilos of water on her head?" And they did that, and they found most of them were suffering from illness in their joints because of carrying that water. And thanks to Ann, there is no way that we would know, because touching a woman is impossible and, you know, it was a hell of a discovery for us.[7]

Figure 7.4 Water march in India.
Source: Photograph by the author

As a woman, I had a rare insight into the women's lives and could convey what I witnessed to Prithvi. He, in turn, believed what I said enough to bring this issue to the attention of the healthcare officials in India. Our circle of trust had led to needed medical attention for the village women.

Stage 11: World Water Day

To honor the Northwestern students' requests to "do something," Prithvi also built some advocacy actions for the students into our schedule. They were able to participate in two large public events—a World Water Day march, led by Maharaja Gaj Singh, and a rally for World Toilet Day. The students were galvanized by their village experiences. One of the students, Andrea, wrote an article about global water issues, which was published in the *Circle of Blue* environmental magazine in the US.[8] The students were starting to use media to enhance their own "water awakening."

Educational Outreach (2010–2012)

When we got back to Chicago, we worked hard to expand the messages learned in India to build more partnerships. We now had international credibility and a video project to show, not tell, about water shortages. New partners joined us who had faith in our current partnerships and in our methods of filming in diverse communities. The trust we had built was scaling up, and the number of our partnerships grew.

Media success followed. Irish musician Bono's ONE.org, which campaigns to end extreme poverty, included our preliminary work on *Water Pressures* in their nationwide campus initiatives on sustainability. MBA and public health programs invited us to present our work, as did broadcasting schools, churches, and national conferences. The Broadcast Educators Association (BEA) invited us to present a panel at their national conference, which reached educators from around the world. We had traction now.

It was time to write the script and find a host for the documentary.

Recruiting a Celebrity for the Work

We needed to find a celebrity host who cared enough about global water issues to take a strong stand on air. I approached several candidates, but Adrian Grenier, a film and TV star, stood out. Adrian was the co-founder of SHFT, a lifestyle platform for sustainable living, whose goal was to save the planet one "shift" at a time. The United Nations had named him an Environment Ambassador, and he'd founded a group called Lonely Whale to protect the seas from all the waste humans threw into it. He understood how important and intertwined global and local water issues and actions were.

Adrian had a true passion about water scarcity that affects the health of millions around the world and spoke with convincing advocacy to young people.

Technical Disaster and Rescue

We had the script and our celebrity host, and we had completed the editing. American Public TV (APT) agreed to syndicate the film nationally to its network of hundreds of public TV stations.

Then, everything came crashing down. The footage that we'd so beautifully shot with so much heart in Rajasthan on our first trip wouldn't sync with the footage shot on our second trip nor with footage shot in the US. The audio wouldn't match up with the video. National Public TV refused to air this mishmash.

How did this happen? I discovered that there were many reasons: our budget was too small to afford top equipment, the video and audio crews who did the three stages of filming didn't consult with each other, and we had a naive belief that we were all "on the same page technically." We weren't.

There was no one I trusted in Chicago to fix this problem, and we were under a severe time crunch—APT planned to air *Water Pressures* in Spring 2013.

I was desperate and turned to the smartest person I knew, Mark Schubin. Mark and his wife Karen were dear friends who had decades of groundbreaking experience in national and international TV production, including *Live from Lincoln Center*, the MET opera, and *Sesame Street*. Mark had been awarded a presidential proclamation award from the Society of Motion Picture and Television Engineers for his five decades of work in the industry.

When I told him about our problems, he dropped everything and urged me to fly to New York City to meet with him and his engineers. My disaster seemed to be mirrored by the weather. I flew into New York on October 27, 2012, just ahead of Hurricane Sandy, the largest hurricane in recorded history to hit the city. I believed in Mark so completely that I literally threw caution to the wind and flew into the storm. When Hurricane Sandy struck, it flooded 51 square miles, knocking out power and shutting down New York City. However, the editing studio at All Mobile Video was on West 26th Street while the power blackout stretched from 25th Street south. Incredibly, we were able to keep working.

At first, Mark's engineer thought that the video and audio problems couldn't be fixed. But Mark sat patiently at his side and made suggestions. Together they came up with solutions to the differing camera and audio speeds we used for filming. Roughly $11,000 later and humbled by this "near failure," I thanked Mark for his help and asked his advice. He said, "The thing to consider: no matter how bad things turned out in the field, it's almost always possible to find some way to fix it."[9]

The lesson hit home: know whom to put your faith in and never give up. That's the crux of building trust, to remain tenaciously optimistic in the face of terrible problems and what looks like certain failure.

Going Public With Water Pressures (April 2013)

American Public Television accepted the beautifully salvaged documentary and broadcast it nationally across the US on Earth Day, April 22, 2013. Nearly 200 public TV stations aired the film and, once again, John McLean Media syndicated the documentary internationally, along with Alexander Press. Our primary corporate sponsor, PepsiCo, showed the documentary in the lobbies of every one of its offices around the world.

The United Nations and PBS Learning Media also used the documentary and its educational guide as part of their program to reach students and communities worldwide with messages of water conservation and partnership. The documentary and its 30-page discussion guide are still in use today.[10]

Lessons Learned

The primary lesson we learned from this six-year project is that the problems of water access and sustainability are far too big for any one country or group to solve. Instead, we need to form global partnerships among countries, governments, corporations, water nonprofits, educational institutions, media, engineers, healthcare specialists, celebrities, and especially young people, who are the ones that will be most impacted by water scarcity.

We also learned that partnerships can succeed only when they're based on mutual respect, value, and trust of one another. Each stakeholder must have an important and unique contribution to make. Global environmental issues are not the place for posturing about power and control. The water crisis gave us the opportunity to collaborate, exchange ideas, create awareness, and unite to solve problems.

The urgency driving our project remains: Water is our most vital resource. It can trigger water wars or forge water alliances. As our documentary *Water Pressures* shows, with compassion, humility, and honesty, we can relieve water pressures on communities and give everyone a future of global water sustainability.

To learn more about the documentary *Water Pressures*, please visit our website at www.buildingcommunitiesoftrust.org

Chapter 7 Case Study: Women and Sanitation in Rural India

Devisha Chandal suffered a dilemma.

At the age of one month, she and 39 other newborns participated in a ceremony led by the elders where each pair—girl and boy—was betrothed to marry at age 18. That was the custom in the Thar Desert, Rajasthan, India.

Devisha was unusually smart and had the good fortune to grow up at just the right time. When she was 11, the local NGO and villagers built a well next to her grade school. The water for the well was used for toilets for the boys and girls. Previously, no girls remained in school through fifth grade, because they needed water to attend to their monthly menstruation. However, Devisha was in the first group of girls who went on not only to graduate eighth grade but also to attend high school. With help from the NGO, she took an hour-long bus ride each day to and from the nearby high school, where she took courses in filmmaking.

Water defined Devisha's life and passion. From a young age, she collected stories which the women told around the nearby water pond, where they congregated each morning and afternoon. At first, she heard stories of the everyday lives of the women, but at one point, the young girl became invisible, and the women started to talk of more serious matters. The women spoke of being harassed when they went out in the dark of night to defecate in nearby wheat fields. One woman was raped by an older man, and the woman's mother-in-law refused to allow her to touch her children, attend to her husband, or even cook meals.

The women had no other choice but to defecate outside. There were no toilets in the village. The ones at the school were locked at night.

Sanitation in Rural India

Sanitation has been a challenge in most of rural India. Specifically, the residents of many villages lack formal toilet facilities, leaving open-air defecation as their only option. Part of the problem is the combination of densely populated areas and diminished groundwater due to increasingly long droughts in the Thar Desert.

As a result, only an estimated one of eight people in rural Rajasthan has access to toilets. Moreover, while sanitation is a recognized world challenge, progress has been slow in coming; advancement in other areas, such as access to clean drinking water, has been more rapid.

Devisha determined to use her filmmaking skills to document the women's stories and improve women's sanitation. At first, the women were shy to share their stories on film, but they knew and trusted her and hoped their stories would help convince the local NGO to build them toilets.

Facing Community Challenges

Devisha's mission was further complicated by social challenges. For example, earlier efforts to modernize the village's sanitation had met with resistance. One of the village elders was especially vocal,

> A group of engineers came and began building toilets without asking our input about their mission. Older residents were confused by how the toilets would work and did not trust the group. Other villagers feared "ghosts" in the toilets and kept them locked for use only by foreign visitors.

The resistance led to the eventual abandonment of the project.

Moreover, differences in gender led to a split in how much support there was to improve sanitation. The men wanted the extra water pipelines used for their crops and livestock. They didn't value the women's fears and objections. And wealthy landowners had their own toilets.

The women whose families had no land were more motivated to work on sanitation projects. The women had multiple reasons to improve sanitation conditions: (1) open-air defecation led to humiliation, and sometimes, even to violence; (2) outdoor defecation was especially challenging in the last stages of pregnancy and during menstruation; and (3) women worried about their children's safety and health for open-air defecation.

Still, despite the women's backing, village residents didn't trust outsiders, especially the European engineering firms which offered to build toilets. Devisha had to help, but how? Then, she came up with an idea: to use her film about women and water to attract support for a World Toilet Day March with the villagers, local NGO and the reigning leaders—the Maharaja and Maharani.

The Project Kicks Off

Devisha shared her 15-minute film with the director of the nearby water NGO. Since the NGO had trained her and supported her through high school, she knew that they shared her passion for helping women find safe solutions for their sanitary needs. The NGO sent the film to the Maharaja and his wife. Maharani Lakshmi Singh took up the women's cause, and with her husband, planned a World Toilet Day March. The intent was to get villagers to sign onto building toilets for the women.

On the day of the March, Devisha stood with the Maharaja and Maharini and filmed the March. Hundreds marched in support.

Questions to Consider

Place yourself in Devisha Chandal's place and consider these questions:

1. What general approach might seem best to offer help to the village regarding its sanitation issues? How active of a role should outside engineering firms take in terms of developing solutions?
2. How should Devisha and the others address some of the community dynamics, such as mistrust about the team project and divisions in the community based on economic class and gender?
3. How can Devisha's advocacy help not only the villagers, but herself? She will soon turn 18 and will marry the local desert boy. She worries that her life as a wife and a mother will keep her away from filmmaking.
4. How can women's and girls' issues regarding sanitation and water be addressed globally? What actions can be taken to ease the water burden on young girls and keep them in school?
5. What follow-up actions can other young students take regarding sanitation issues even though they don't live in the desert? Should they act locally, globally, or some combination of the two?

Notes

1 www.cdc.gov/healthywater/global/wash_statistics.html.
2 Ibid.
3 Dan Bena, interview with Ann Feldman, December 12, 2019.
4 Congresswoman Jan Schakowsky, interview with Ann Feldman, November 25, 2019.
5 Prithvi Raj Singh, interview with Ann Feldman, February 19, 2019.
6 Yuri Malina's email to William Natale, Director, *Water Pressures*, January 2019.
7 Raj Singh, op.cit.
8 Andrea Hart, www.circleofblue.org/2010/world/standing-in-a-long-really-long-line-toilet-queue-serves-indian-village-effort-to-promote-sanitation-awareness/.
9 Mark Schubin, interview with Ann Feldman, April 3, 2019.
10 To learn more about the documentary Water Pressures, please visit our website at www.buildingcommunitiesoftrust.org.

References

1. Ahmed, Sara, ed. "Why Is Gender Equity a Concern for Water Management?" and "SEWA: Campaigning for Water, Women and Work." In: *Flowing Upstream: Empowering Women Through Water Management Initiatives*

in India. Cambridge, MA: Cambridge University Press, 2005, 1–50, 93–122. Online 2011.

2. Annin, Peter. *The Great Lakes Water Wars*. Washington, DC: Island Press, 2006.
3. Barlow, Maude. *Whose Water Is It Anyway?: Taking Water Protection into Public Hands*. Toronto, Canada: ECW Press, 2019.
4. Fagen, Brian. *Elixir: A History of Water and Humankind*. London: Bloomsbury Press, 2011.
5. Fishman, Charles. *The Big Thirst: The Secret Life and Turbulent Future of Water*. Glencoe, IL: Free Press, 2011.
6. Kolb, David. *Experiential Learning: Experience as the Source of Learning and Development*. Englewood Cliffs, NJ: Prentice Hall, 1984.
7. Ostrom, Elinor. *Governing the Commons: The Evolution of Institutions for Collective Action*. Cambridge, MA: Cambridge University Press, 1990.
8. Pearce, Fred. *When the Rivers Run Dry: The Defining Crisis of the Twenty-First Century*. Boston, MA: Beacon Press, 2007.
9. Prud'homme, Alex. *The Ripple Effect: The Fate of Fresh Water in the Twenty-First Century*. New York: Scribner & Sons, 2011.
10. Gleick, Peter H., Heather Cooley, Michael J. Cohen, Mari Morikawa, Jason Morrison and Meena Palaniappan. "Peak Water." In: *The World's Water: 2008–2009 Biennial Report on Freshwater Resources*. Washington, DC: Island Press, 2009. www.worldwater.org/data20082009/ch01.pdf.

8   Save Yourself

Trauma and Mindfulness:
Pause and Shift Directions
When Your Life and Work Hit
Major Obstacles

It's one thing to learn to trust others. It's another to trust and care for
yourself, especially during serious health challenges. For those of us
whose life's purpose is to produce creative work for social change,
it's heart-breaking to think we can no longer contribute. However, we
can reimagine other ways to contribute to the public good. My way
was through writing this book, asking for insights from our partners,
and creating case studies with college students to help them develop
key strategies for building their own communities of trust.

Every project we created over 30 years was linked to *Tikkun Olam*, the Jewish practice of repairing the world. However, for our final project, things
became a lot more personal as I faced a major health crisis. The project's
focus grew out of my own personal challenges.

Building My Own Communities of Trust for Health
(2012–2021)

In 2012, as we edited the final master for the *Water Pressures* documentary,
I noticed an enlarged node on my left groin. After a PET scan, I learned that
I had Stage Four Non-Hodgkin's Lymphoma. Stage Four is the final stage.
It doesn't get much worse than that.

   To survive the upcoming medical ordeal, I built my own communities of
trust for my physical and mental health. I found doctors on whom I could
rely, concerned survivors with superb advice, and a wider network of vision-
aries who explored the links between trauma and disease. What started as a
personal crisis became our next media project dealing with the relationship
of trauma and mindfulness.

DOI: 10.4324/9781003296423-9

The first person I learned to trust was Jenna Benn Shersher, a friend of my younger daughter. Jenna had beaten the rare Grey's Zone Lymphoma with the help of Dr. Leo Gordon, a lymphoma specialist at Northwestern University Medical Center in Chicago. Though Dr. Gordon had a very busy practice, Jenna helped me get in to see him. Dr. Gordon looked over my medical records and, to my surprise, wasn't too concerned: "You'll live a long life with this disease, and it won't be fatal. When and if it gets problematic, there are excellent treatments to slow it down." He advised that I follow a measured "wait and see" approach.

While his words gave me hope, it was Jenna who taught me how to fight cancer, not succumb to it. Jenna was the Founder and Director of Twist Out Cancer, an international organization that mobilized cancer survivors and their supporters to live through cancer with beauty and confidence.

Jenna had an aggressive attitude. She told me that she visualized cancer "as a dirty whore, who was just everywhere, uninvited, stealing moments and experiences from me." Jenna imagined "going to war against the cancer whore: Sometimes in the boxing ring, sometimes in the trenches, and sometimes it was me against her on a basketball court. Metaphorically, I was constantly kicking the crap out of her."[1]

My images were different, gentler, but equally as effective. I imagined Superhero Enrique and his crew cheerfully going throughout my body with their mops, Lysol, and magic formulas, cleaning away the lymphoma and restoring my body to renewed health.

However, as I battled the cancer, disturbing images of childhood abuse surfaced. Memories of the mental and physical abuse I'd experienced turned out to be harder to fight than the cancer. For spiritual guidance, I turned to my Buddhist teacher, Geshe Gendun Gyatso, a Tibetan monk.

Geshe advised me to follow the compassion practices of mindfulness and meditation. As a Tibetan growing up in exile in India, those were the values instilled by *his* teacher, the Dalai Lama, who asserted that "human nature is compassionate." However, Geshe viewed Americans differently:

> The American point of view is that time is money. The value is money. There is nothing about compassion, which doesn't mean anything of value. So, your compassion is on the action level. Lots of people talk about compassion. But on the action level, they're not doing it.

Geshe's statement went right to the core of my greatest worry—that I might not be able to finish my life's work, to continue to be of service to others. Geshe offered to help me turn that worry into action. We decided to explore the connection between trauma and disease and to create a TV documentary about mindfulness and trauma. Millions of other people must

Figure 8.1 Buddhist monk praying.

Source: Photograph with permission from Geshe Gendun Gyatso Konchhok

be facing the same thing I was, in one form or another. What had started as a personal issue became a universal one.

While our documentary project didn't really fit Artistic Circles' mission to showcase women, the arts, and social change, still, it was true to my heart and personal experiences. Fortunately, Artistic Circles' board of directors and our funders supported my exploration of this difficult and important topic.

Trauma and Trust: Washington State (2013–2014)

We decided to start our film with people who were experts in childhood traumas and their health effects. The Centers for Disease Control had a program called Adverse Childhood Experiences (ACEs). This group identified connections between late-onset diseases and early childhood traumas. We filmed ACEs experts talking about trauma intervention programs for young kids and the positive impact their work had on the lives of children.

Their approach seemed to click with Artistic Circles' emphasis on building trust. It's a sad fact that children in abusive homes can't trust their parents and don't know whom to turn to for help. ACES had built a brilliant intervention program into the fabric of school life in Washington State. That model, with the added reach of our television documentary, could help other students, families, and schools around the country.

The Challenge of Filming When There's Little Trust

The ACES team told us about one of their trauma intervention programs in the Washington grade schools, a program overseen by a local university and their director. I contacted the director, who invited me and the film crew to videotape their successful grade-school interventions. The film crew and I were excited to showcase this innovative program.

However, we encountered unexpected resistance. The first night we arrived, the university director sternly told us, "If you make this film about me, I'll ruin you. But don't forget, I raised all the money for the programs, and I'm in charge." This was a classic case of "pull you in, push you away," a situation that got worse as we started filming in the schools.

We found that the grade schools themselves were a model of mindfulness, including morning hugs by the principal and teachers as students entered the school, counseling outside the classroom, and free meals for poorer students on weekends. We got great interviews with principals, teachers, students, and parents, who were happy to have us showcase their programs. Unfortunately, there was always a university "minder" with us, a young woman who shadowed our work. She was a master's student at the university, who reported back daily to the director of the program. The "minder" kept interfering with our filming and interviews.

One day she went too far. She accused a member of our crew of lying and being mean to the students. Then, she told a school principal that we were illegally filming the students' faces, thereby violating their privacy. This was a bald lie. I not only showed the principal the footage, which followed all legal requirements, but also talked with the university director and told him to call off the "minder." Things had gotten out of hand.

Erik Gulbrandsen, our editor, recalls:

> The university people were always suspicious, wondering, what are these people up to? Like we were an investigative film crew for the news show 20/20, doing some kind of an exposé. There was a "minder" with us at all times, watching us. We found the paranoia to be really strange. It's not what I expected from people who are supposedly using mindfulness and meditation to deal with mental issues and addiction.[2]

We had assumed from our work with ACEs that institutional mindfulness meant the leadership would be enlightened. The resistance and suspicion from the university director was unnerving. Nevertheless, we forged ahead with the help of teachers, principals, counselors, and parents. The best experiences we had were "off the grid." One of the public health nurses, Melissa Charbonneau, arranged for us to interview a student, Joseph, and his mother at their trailer home.

Joseph had been troubled and violent, and his mother worried that he would end up in jail or dead. That's when she turned to Melissa and the school counseling program for help. We hoped to capture Joseph's story on film. At the beginning, Melissa remembered:

> I really had to push myself in working with them. I was scared, so, I just imagined how scared this mom was. That's what made me suck it up and forge ahead. Joseph's mom learned to trust me over time.

> Your camera people, sound people, you, the whole crew were great to work with and had a way to calm my nerves. I could feel the passion you have in working with others and telling their stories.[3]

Melissa showed us that while trust and fear can be linked, trust can also overcome fear. By creating a partnership with Melissa, Joseph, and his mother, we put together a short, powerful video (https://vimeo.com/

Figure 8.2 Boy, mother, and psychologist.
Source: Photograph by the author

manage/videos/144719283—password:cigarettebaby). Through the ACEs work, and with Melissa's help, Joseph was able to stay in school and avoid the downward spiral that his life would otherwise have taken.

When the university leadership learned that we'd filmed without their minder present, they were furious, and everything fell apart. They wanted to control our crew, dictate what and whom we could film, and restrict what stories we'd tell. In contrast, our crew and I wanted to let the students, teachers, principals, and parents tell their *own* stories.

Knowing When to Walk Away

We had arrived at a complete impasse with the university. This was the moment of choice for us. Would we continue filming and rely on the fragile trust we had built with the teachers, parents, students, and counselors or simply walk away? The crew and I discussed the costs, both in terms of money and ethics, for us to continue. The local schools relied on the university to bring in national funding for the trauma intervention program. We didn't want to endanger their funding or their relationship with the university. We followed the dictum, "Do no harm," and packed up our equipment and left.

We weren't willing to give up on our idea of filming trauma and mindfulness stories, so we had extensive conversations with the military about mindfulness, yoga, and PTSD; with sports franchises about mindfulness and excellence; and with colleges and universities about mindfulness and trauma initiatives on campuses. Nothing seemed to click.

What was going on? I knew from experience that timing and having the correct partners can make or break a project. But despite our best efforts, we had neither for this stage of the work. In addition, we had strayed too far from Artistic Circles' core strength, which focused on women and the arts. Instead, we had ventured into the realm of trauma, which is loaded with pitfalls. Perhaps we weren't having any success because we tackled a topic too far out of our wheelhouse of expertise.

It was a good thing that I listened to my intuition, because it freed me to devote my energies to an unexpected turn in my health.

Trust and Care: Know Your Limits

In the fall of 2014, I had a bicycle accident and fractured my hip. During a partial hip replacement operation, the doctor found extensive lymphoma in my bones, indicating that the cancer had become more aggressive. That meant that I would need half-day infusions of cancer-fighting drugs at the hospital on a monthly basis. As those treatments continued through 2014, my attitude about the documentary changed.

I needed to protect myself and remove all stress from my life. Filming a documentary in a controversial environment like Spokane was exhausting. Plus, the additional tasks of raising money, managing a crew, and looking for media outlets were too hard on my psyche and my body. I had reached my limit and was ready to set boundaries to protect both my mental and physical health.

Writing Building Communities of Trust *(2015)*

With no documentary to work on, I needed a positive outlet, a way to keep repairing the world despite being stuck in my home after surgery and treatment. I'd always written the scripts for our documentaries but hadn't really written for pure pleasure. In early 2015, I started taking writing classes and experimenting with storytelling through fiction and nonfiction. The nonfiction stories I wanted to share focused on lessons learned during our 30 years of creating communities of trust around the world. For the first time, I wanted to include stories of the hiccups, confrontations, and failures we'd never told publicly. Did I have the courage to share those painful stories to help others create their own social-impact projects?

The idea of writing this book was born, but I would need others' help to accomplish it. In Spring 2015, I turned to our project partners for assistance. What did they recall about the successes and failures of our work together? Where did we get it right, and what did we do to recover when we got it wrong? What lessons could be shared with future leaders? I ended up placing these interviews throughout this book to provide other viewpoints and voices regarding our work.

As a cultural historian, I realized that the next step was to analyze Artistic Circles' history. Just as we'd diligently researched women heroes of the Chicago World's Fair for our first project, so a team and I went back through 30 years of Day-Timers, Journals, media programs, letters, emails, and documents to find the most vibrant lessons that emerged from those projects.

The main lesson that stood out for us was *learning to build communities of trust*. That was our motivation, the foundation for each program, and the way we judged the success or failure of our efforts. How many trusting partnerships had we managed to build and maintain through each project? The team leaders I interviewed shared this moral compass point.

Involving the Students

One of the largest communities of trust we had built for our projects was with undergraduate and graduate students. For decades, I'd hired college interns from Northwestern University to help create and evaluate our projects. For

Figure 8.3 College students in discussion.

Source: Photograph by the author

this book, these interns helped organize roundtable discussions with their colleagues. One conversation focused on strategies they could use to save themselves when their identities were threatened.

Undergraduate students at Northwestern University talked about what works and what doesn't after leaving home to live at college. Kaisha told us that she had lost her religious faith when she came to college, which triggered arguments with her parents who were both pastors. Her community of friends supported her as she found ways to create a new identity.

In 2020, I returned to academia for the missing piece that this book needed—case studies at the end of each chapter. The goal was to take the lessons we had learned with each project and transform them into problems the students would solve in their own creative ways. We hoped that it would encourage students to come up with their *own* solutions to the social, moral, environmental, spiritual, and psychological issues they would face.

In partnership with Sachin Waikar, Ph.D., a former financial strategist, clinical psychologist, and acclaimed writer, we created these case studies. Carol Zsolnay, a former member of the management team at Northwestern's Kellogg School of Management, consulted with us.

Glasgow Caledonian College in New York agreed to test-market the *Water Pressures* chapter and case study for their graduate course, "Leadership and

Strategy." The Director of Social Impact, Dr. Gaston de los Reyes, invited me to present these materials to his students in April 2021. We trusted the students to tell us whether our idea would work.

Through breakout sessions and written feedback, the students taught us how best to use the book's chapters and case studies. Their suggestions included:

- The activities need to be tied back to everyone in the classroom. How does this affect us? Is this a call to action? Can we use these lessons in our future careers?
- The author can focus on the conflicts that arose during the projects and how they were successfully resolved.
- We were stimulated that the problems in the chapters came out of a human ethical dilemma as a consequence of "doing good." It raised nuanced questions about how the line between "help" and "interference" isn't always clear.
- The chapter and case study helped us put ourselves in the decision-making position. How would we solve such problems when pursuing this type of endeavor?[4]

Final Lessons: Trust and Social Change

Through health and illness, success and failure, travel to far-flung places and being tethered at home, my goal has always been to improve life for others and, ultimately, for myself. I chose broad tools—TV, radio, videos, CDs, public forums, books, and articles—to amplify the universal message: be courageous and compassionate in dealing with people who are different from ourselves. By taking risks and treating people equitably by telling their stories, we help make the world a more compassionate and loving place.

We reached millions of people with our media projects, but it turned out that I was the one most changed by these experiences. The work helped open my heart and renew my vigor to repair the world.

Today, we are living in a time of unprecedented challenges, including COVID-19 and its variants, conflict in many parts of the world, climate change, and moral reckoning, as shown by movements such as Black Lives Matter and #MeToo. Faced with such uncertainty and change, many are searching for a new path of peace and well-being. We are essentially searching for TRUST.

What is trust? Here's what I've learned through our projects:

- Trust means being at peace with your partners despite whatever turmoil you go through and finding joy and challenges in their presence.

- The keys to building that trust are mutual respect and curiosity toward one another.
- Building trust is like putting money in the bank that you can draw on when things become difficult and threaten to fall apart.
- Trust means a shared responsibility for keeping the balance. The "good" and "bad" of every project are shared among all parties.
- **And most important of all,** trust means creating a safe space for individuals and communities to make positive social changes.

I've relied on building communities of trust not only for my work but also for my health. Eleven years after my initial diagnosis of Non-Hodgkin's Lymphoma, I live life to the fullest and am in excellent health. Every day, I walk two miles, swim, and do bands and weights. I eat healthy and enjoy family and friends (sometimes in person and other times by Zoom). I've learned to appreciate every single minute of every day. I've also learned to distance myself from people and projects that tear me down instead of build me up. This book built me up, because I have the privilege of engaging with so many.

May this book encourage you to build your own communities of trust and find ways to help repair the world through your work.

Chapter 8 Case Study: Dilemma and Choice

Brian Chan faced a dilemma about his work and life.

On paper, the 25-year-old was in an enviable position: he was in his fourth, highly successful year at a major US strategy consulting firm, based in San Francisco. He had proven to be an adept problem-solver, strong communicator, and rising leader, earning a rare promotion to Senior Analyst. His annual salary already exceeded $100,000/year.

The Costs of Others' Expectations

But there was a big problem.

As Brian's responsibilities with the firm had grown, so did the hours he spent at work. Of course, his work had many benefits. His large salary helped him pay off college loans, and he had high status among peers, and a supportive community of colleagues.

However, all this came at a steep personal cost to Brian's personal life. His girlfriend left him, he rarely saw his friends, and often had to miss his favorite outside activity, volunteering at an animal shelter. His health was also beginning to suffer. He had lost weight, had trouble sleeping, and was always tired, often struggling to concentrate.

Making a change was not so simple. Brian wanted to please his parents and extended family. His parents had immigrated from China in the 1990s and were excited about their only son's career success. His parents' move to the US before Brian's birth had involved a great sacrifice. They had been young professionals in China, but in the US, they had to take on more menial jobs initially, as a dishwasher and house cleaner. In addition, Brian was now a hero to his larger family and regularly sent money back to China to support aunts, uncles, and cousins.

The full weight of family expectations fell on Brian as a male, first-generation Chinese American. Brian felt guilty about burdening his parents with his increasing doubts about work. He also recognized that he had become accustomed to a high-status, high-paying career, despite its personal costs.

A Difficult Choice to Make

Things had come to a head recently when Brian started working on an important technology assignment with a very tight schedule. His team was putting in 15-hour days to meet the deadline. Even with this workload, Brian had been given time off to attend his favorite cousin's wedding that weekend.

But by mid-week, Brian's manager told him everyone needed to work the entire weekend, no exceptions. Work, family, friends, and personal needs collided as Brian wrestled with missing his cousin's wedding.

There was more at stake than simply attending the ceremony. One of his older friends, a veterinarian, was going to be there as well. The two of them had often talked about Brian's love of animals and the possibility he could switch careers and pursue a veterinarian degree. In fact, his friend even suggested that they could talk at the wedding about how Brian could help manage her practice while he attended veterinarian school.

With the wedding just days away, Brian thought about the future life he wanted to have. How could he manage a balance between work and personal life and still satisfy his parents' expectations and his own? He wanted a wife and family and had to think about the effect his professional life would have on that dream. Should he remain a business consultant or start on the path to become a veterinarian?

Questions to Consider

Put yourself in Brian's position as you consider the dilemma he faces.

1. What issues do you believe characterize the challenges in Brian's life? Based on your experience and that of others you know, how common is the predicament he faces?

2. In considering his dilemma, what advice would you give Brian?
3. What practical steps can Brian take to learn what attending veterinarian school would require, and how best to switch careers?
4. Whom do you think Brian should ask for advice: parents, mentors, friends, a financial advisor, and experts in business and veterinary medicine?
5. How does Brian's situation relate to decisions you might be facing in your own life regarding the balance of career, personal pursuits, money, and family/community expectations?

Notes

1 Jenna Benn Shersher, videotaped interview with Ann Feldman, July 9, 2012.
2 Erik Gulbrandsen, interview with Ann Feldman, April 11, 2019.
3 Melissa Charbonneau, in an email to Ann Feldman, August 19, 2019.
4 Gaston de los Reyes, from a July 19, 2021, email to Ann Feldman that included written feedback from GCNYC students enrolled in his "Leadership and Strategy" class, Spring and Summer 2021.

References

ACES Bibliography

1. Felitti, Vincent J. "The Relation Between Adverse Childhood Experiences and Adult Health: Turning Gold into Lead." *The Permanente Journal*, Winter 2002, Vol. 6, No. 1, 44–47.
2. Tough, Paul. *How Children Succeed: Grit, Curiosity and the Hidden Power of Character*. Boston: Mariner Books, 2013.
3. Institute for Safe Families. *The National Summit on Adverse Childhood Experiences*. Philadelphia, PA: Institute for Safe Families, May 14, 2013.
4. A Video Series on *The ACE Study*. Hove: Cavalcade Productions, Inc., 2005.
5. Davidson, Richard and Sharon Begley. *The Emotional Life of Your Brain*. New York: Avery Publishing, 2012.

Index

Milton Keynes UK
Ingram Content Group UK Ltd.
UKHW022041190124
436364UK00007B/67